The Alchemist
All for Love
Arden of Faversham
The Atheist's Tragedy
Bartholmew Fair
The Beaux' Stratagem
The Broken Heart
Bussy D'Ambois
The Changeling
A Chaste Maid in Cheapside
The Country Wife
The Critic
The Devil's Law-Case
The Double-Dealer
Dr Faustus
The Duchess of Malfi
The Dutch Courtesan
Eastward Ho!
Edward the Second
Epicoene or The Silent Woman
Every Man In His Humour
A Fair Quarrel
Gammer Gurton's Needle
An Ideal Husband
The Importance of Being Earnest
The Jew of Malta
The Knight of the Burning Pestle
Lady Windermere's Fan
London Assurance
Love for Love
The Malcontent
The Man of Mode

Marriage A-la-Mode
A New Way to Pay Old Debts
The Old Wife's Tale
The Plain Dealer
The Playboy of the Western World
The Provoked Wife
The Recruiting Officer
The Relapse
The Revenger's Tragedy
The Rivals
The Roaring Girl
The Rover
The School for Scandal
She Stoops to Conquer
The Shoemaker's Holiday
The Spanish Tragedy
Tamburlaine
Three Late Medieval Morality Plays
    Mankind
    Everyman
    Mundus et Infans
Thyestes
'Tis Pity She's a Whore
Volpone
The Way of the World
The White Devil
The Witch
The Witch of Edmonton
A Woman Killed with Kindness
A Woman of No Importance
Women Beware Women

NEW MERMAIDS

General Editor: Brian Gibbons
Professor of English Literature, University of Münster

The interior of a Restoration theatre
drawn by C. Walter Hodges

William Congreve

Love for Love

editcd by Malcolm Kelsall

Professor of English, University of Wales, Cardiff

A & C Black • London
W W Norton • New York

Second edition 1999
A & C Black (Publishers) Limited
35 Bedford Row, London WC1R 4JH
ISBN 0–7136–4323–4

© 1998 A & C Black (Publishers) Limited

First New Mermaid edition published 1969
by Ernest Benn Limited
© 1969 Ernest Benn Limited

Published in the United States of America
by W. W. Norton and Company, Inc.
500 Fifth Avenue, New York, N.Y. 10110
ISBN 0–393–90084–3

CIP catalogue records for this book
are available from the British Library
and the Library of Congress.

Printed in Great Britain by
Whitstable Litho Printers Ltd,
Whitstable, Kent

CONTENTS

ACKNOWLEDGEMENTS

In editing the text I have made much use of Montague Summers's edition of *The Complete Works of William Congreve* (London, The Nonesuch Press, 1923), whose annotations are the fullest available, and the edition, by my much respected teacher and friend, the late Herbert Davis, of Congreve's *Complete Plays* (Chicago, University of Chicago Press, 1967). Davis's text is based on extensive collation in England and the United States of the authoritative editions published in Congreve's lifetime. The textual apparatus printed here substantially corresponds with his, but further collation has enabled me to add to the list of variants. I am also indebted to the editions of Anthony G. Henderson, *The Comedies of William Congreve* (Cambridge, Cambridge University Press, 1982), Eric S. Rump, *The Comedies of William Congreve* (Harmondsworth, Penguin Books, 1985) and Emmett L. Avery, *Love for Love* (London, Edward Arnold, 1967). Since the first New Mermaid edition was published in 1969, my own experience in teaching in Britain, Asia, Europe and the United States has shown that more substantial annotation is required than was initially judged to be appropriate. I have taken the opportunity, therefore, to increase and revise the explanatory apparatus.

University of Wales   MALCOLM KELSALL
Cardiff

INTRODUCTION

The Author

William Congreve was born at Bardsey in Yorkshire on 24 January 1670.[1] He was educated in Ireland where his father went first as lieutenant in a company of foot, and later became resident agent for the Earl of Cork and Burlington. At Kilkenny College school he was a younger contemporary of Jonathan Swift, and from thence went, like Swift, to Trinity College, Dublin. He was enrolled 17 March 1691 as a law student in the Middle Temple, London.

Congreve had little intention of studying law. At Will's coffee house, Covent Garden, he became the associate of many of the leading literary figures of the day, in particular John Dryden, to whose translation of Juvenal and Persius (1693) he contributed a version of Juvenal's eleventh satire. His first comedy, *The Old Bachelor*, was produced at Drury Lane in March 1693. Dryden, who had helped in its preparation for the stage, called it the best first play he had seen; Thomas Southerne, the dramatist, recommended it to Thomas Davenant, the manager of the Theatre Royal; it ran for the unusual length for those times of fourteen days. This was followed by *The Double Dealer* in December of the same year, *Love for Love* (1695), *The Mourning Bride*, a tragedy (1697), *The Way of the World* (1700), and a masque, *The Judgment of Paris* (1701). This was Congreve's last work as a playwright.[2] Although his plays were soon established in the standard repertory, it has been said that Congreve gave up the theatre because he was disappointed in his public. Despite the immediate success of *The Old Bachelor* and *Love for Love*, his other comedies were at first caviare to the general. *The Double Dealer* only just escaped being hissed from the stage, his finest achievement, *The Way of the World*, was said not to 'answer expectation'; to be too keen in its satire to win general applause. But it has also been claimed that there was nothing further for him to achieve in comedy. He knew when his vein was exhausted; he had perfected his art in *The Way of the World* and his love of ease was greater than his ambition. 'Ease and quiet is

---

[1] The biographical information in this section is from J. C. Hodges, *William Congreve the Man: a Biography from New Sources* (New York, Modern Language Association of America, 1941).

[2] Other works include *Incognita*, a novel (1692), *An Essay Concerning Humour in Comedy* (1696), *Amendments of Mr. Collier's False and Imperfect Citations* (1698) and *Semele,* an opera printed in 1710.

what I hunt after,' he wrote. 'If I have not ambition, I have other passions more easily gratified.'

He lived thereafter as Voltaire described him 'upon no other foot than that of a gentleman, who led a life of plainness and simplicity.'[3] He was not rich. His government sinecures did not pay well until, after the accession of George I, his Whig friends obtained him a commission as Secretary to the Island of Jamaica; his speculation with Vanbrugh as joint manager of the new Haymarket theatre (1704–5) was a failure; his share in Betterton's company in Lincoln's Inn Fields proved of little value. He was, however, the friend of the wits and of the great. He was one of the group which met initially (at the expense of Tonson, the publisher) to consume the mutton pies of Christopher Cat in Sheer Lane, from whence the Kit-Cat club grew. He was thus acquainted with Addison, Steele, Kneller and Vanbrugh; he was a friend of Swift and Pope, who dedicated his translation of the *Iliad* to him, and of Lady Mary Wortley Montagu; he was the lover of Henrietta, Duchess of Marlborough, with whom much of his time in his declining years was spent. He died 19 January 1729 and was buried in Westminster Abbey.

The Play
(and Its Critics)

No account of *Love for Love* can be definitive for it is inevitably part of an ongoing argument about Congreve in particular and the social function of theatre in general. One may merely locate the current position in that history. The general context of the debate is as old as Plato. It concerns the uncertain relationship between art and morality. In Congreve's lifetime the issue was polarised by Jeremy Collier's *A Short View of the Immorality, and Profaneness of the English Stage, Together with the Sense of Antiquity upon this Argument* (1698). For Collier, the comic drama of his own age was the prime target and Congreve's plays a gross example of immoral profanity. Although Collier was an extremist, the tide of public opinion was flowing in his direction. It was a slow process, but appreciation of Restoration comedy had withered and died by the early nineteenth century. The moral blasts of Collier still blew in the Podsnappery of Thomas Babington Macaulay. Mr. Podsnap (in Dickens's *Our Mutual Friend*) believed that literature should never 'bring a blush into the cheek of the young person', and Congreve was removed from the canon of live theatre as not morally correct.

In the twentieth century, with the rise of 'English Literature' as an

---

[3] *Letters Concerning the English Nation*, XIX.

academic subject, the return of Congreve to the canon revived the moral issue. A new astringent scrutiny in the University of Cambridge weighed Congreve in the balance against the mature comedy of Henry James, and found Congreve wanting. Compared with modern writers like D. H. Lawrence, who have explored the relationship between the sexes in new depth, Congreve's moral vision was found to be superficial and cliché-ridden. He was, like his period, 'gross, trivial and dull'.[4] Lamb's defence of the comedy of the Restoration, that because it is a world of high fantasy it is outside moral consideration, has had little support.[5] Those who sought to restore Congreve as a serious writer for academic study claimed that his work was a mirror of the times, and when this provoked the obvious rejoinder that his was merely a fragmented and superficial culture, the major names of the philosophers Hobbes and Locke have been evoked. The comedies have been seen as pursuing that union of judgement and fancy which is true wit, or as seeking (even epistemologically) for some basis of value in personal relations in a deceptive and corrupt society.[6] The moral case has been pushed to extremes. In contradistinction to Collier, the plays have been interpreted as a (secular) Christian allegory. Providence is vindicated by the happy ending of comedies (and the heroine of *Love for Love* is called Angelica).[7]

But such has been the rapidity of change in the academic study of 'English Literature', that what were the 'standard' critical texts even ten years ago are now becoming merely part of the history of criticism. The rise of 'critical and cultural theory' has radically changed the subjects and terminology of criticism of drama. Although the main thrust of the new agenda in the academic world in general has been directed towards Shakespeare, everywhere it opens a division between plays as theatrecraft (which would be seen as a mere aesthetic evasion or humanist mystification) and plays as 'text' and 'text' as ideological discourse to be judged in terms of gender, class and race.

The dichotomy has become especially contentious because of the development, in some quarters, of the hegemonic and totalising pre-

---

[4] Knights (1946).

[5] Charles Lamb, 'On the Artificial Comedy of the Last Age', in *The Essays of Elia* (1821).

[6] Fujimura (1952). Norman Holland's (1959) concern with appearance and nature initiated a series of 'mimetic' investigations of the relation of comedy as a genre to its intellectual and social milieu – in general Donaldson (1970), Hawkins (1972) – and more specifically Novak (1971) who saw Congreve set between a passing age of 'wit' and a new age of 'sentiment', a view to which Hume (1976) added strong support.

[7] Williams (1979).

tensions of cultural criticism. It is not merely a matter of a change of critical agenda, therefore, although there has been an historical change. (Thus, questions of gender identity raised by current feminisms appear now more pertinent to *Love for Love* than the moral concerns of F. R. Leavis which were prevalent in the 1960s, and current understanding of history would be more likely to examine the play rather in terms of the discourses of power it reveals than in relation to the concern of the 60s with transhistorical myth.) But the new agenda, in its extreme manifestations, claims to be not an alternative form of interpretation in an historical process, but the only form. The claim is that everything signifies ideologically, and thus everything is part of an ideological battleground. The plays of Shakespeare and a cornflakes packet are both 'texts' (so Terence Hawkes has argued)[8] and thus both material for the cultural critic to contest.

There is no innocent theatrecraft, therefore. Even those aspects of recent theory which might have liberated theatre from ideology have been recruited for politicised purposes. The idea of 'carnival', for instance, is fundamental in comic play, for changing costume and turning the world topsy-turvy is a practice as old as theatre itself. But these elements of 'carnival' have been interpreted (from the theories of the Marxist Mikhail Bakhtin) as part of discourses of social protest and social control. So, Mrs. Bracegirdle in breeches about to deliver the (rejected) Prologue for *Love for Love*, might be read as signifying (semiotically) transgressive proto-feminism, and Sir Sampson as an arbitrary representative of 'the patriarchy'.[9] If, in reaction to the remorseless processes of ideological interpretation, one might point out that even the Marxist Brecht claimed that one goes to the theatre to have fun (a view Dickens's circus-master Mr. Sleary in *Hard Times* would endorse) yet, still, the academic theorist has an ideological agenda even for fun. (S)he, with an obeisance to Roland Barthes, would distinguish now between that *plaisir*

---

[8] *The Mail on Sunday* 5 March 1995. The extreme ideological position has entirely excluded theatre as a subject from a representative work like *The Toronto Encyclopedia of Contemporary Literary Theory* (Toronto, Toronto University Press, 1993).

[9] Congreve's Whig affiliations are well established. Sir Sampson's arbitrary views are a parody of Stuart 'absolutism', and Congreve, as a Whig, would subscribe to a doctrine of free contract between subjects and rulers which would extend to the contractual relationship between men and women in marriage. But 'heavy' fathers and rebellious children are as old as theatrical comedy itself, and Congreve's witty and independent heroines are directly derived from Shakespeare's articulate comic heroines.

which is socially conservative and the greater *jouissance* which is radical.

Thus a 'new' Mermaid edition of *Love for Love* is apposite now because the whole agenda of criticism has changed since the last edition in 1969. It is apposite also because of the emphasis in the New Mermaids on play as theatrecraft.[10] A play-text (as things are now) has acquired two separable modes of existence: either as a discourse through which the cultural critic may reveal the text's (or the critic's) ideology,[11] or as pure theatrecraft embodied and voiced by actors on stage. That crude dichotomy is not unbridgeable, of course, but the two modes of interpretation are now radically divided. The history of *Love for Love* as 'the play on the stage' which follows cannot be neutral in this context, therefore. On the contrary it is embattled against a dominant mode of critical interpretation.

On the other hand, no theatrical practitioner would reject the idea that everything on stage signifies (theatre folk have been practising 'semiotics' for millennia without being theoretically aware – like M. Jourdain in Molière's *Le Bourgeois Gentilhomme* who eventually learnt from theory that he was speaking prose). Likewise, any performer is crucially and continually aware of a direct and immediate relation between the spoken or sung text and the culture in which the text is performed. It could not be more direct. The point of contact is the audience (or spectators – English has no word which encompasses the audio-visual relationship). Actor and audience are always aware of the 'applicability' of plays (to use a seventeenth-century word), whether to major issues (such as the Popish Plot) or to everyday trivia (fashonable eating houses). There is, accordingly, a bridge between 'play' and 'culture', 'craft' and 'theory', but it is a bridge between two separable continents. What follows is an attempt to cross that bridge, although the passage between the two is, perhaps, not available to those who would refuse to distinguish *Hamlet* from a cornflakes packet.

---

[10] Scholarly understanding of Restoration theatre has, in large measure, developed independently of ideological criticism. I am particularly indebted to Love (1974), Peter Holland (1979), Powell (1984) and above all to Styan (1986). Styan's understanding of language, character and action has given scholarly weight to what were the intuitive interpretations of the original introduction to this edition in 1969.

[11] The discourse of Congreve (ideologised theoretically) would be seen as characterised by its commitment to the 'Gramscian' hegemonic apparatus of the Whig establishment post 1688. It would form, in general, part of the print culture of the 'Habermasian' bourgeois public sphere, and, probably, is implicated (by gender) with the widely diffused misogyny of patriarchal culture in the seventeenth century. The beginning of this kind of reading may be seen developmentally in Markley (1980), Peter (1990), Gill (1994) and Canfield (1995).

The Play on the Stage

Love for Love was finished before the end of 1694, but not performed until 30 April 1695, when it ran for thirteen days.[12] The delay in production was largely occasioned by a quarrel within the 'United Company' at the Theatre Royal between the actors and the patentees. Thomas Betterton, the foremost actor of the company, broke with the patentees, and having secured a licence, established a new playhouse in Lincoln's Inn Fields, carrying with him a substantial number of the principal players from the Theatre Royal. *Love for Love* was chosen to open the new house. According to Colley Cibber it 'ran on with such extraordinary success, that they had seldom occasion to act any other play, till the end of the season.'[13] Betterton (although in his sixties) acted Valentine; Anne Bracegirdle, the famous beauty, was well suited to Angelica; the great Elizabeth Barry, for whom Otway had created his most famous roles, now no longer in the flower of youth, was cast as Mrs. Frail; Samuel Sandford, a man 'diminutive, and mean, (being round-shouldered, meagre-faced, spindle-shanked, splay-footed, with a sour countenance, and long lean arms)', was chosen as Foresight. The greatest success, however, was achieved by Thomas Dogget as Ben, who, it was said, had taken lodgings in Wapping to get up his sailor's part at first hand.[14]

An account of 'the play on stage' must begin tentatively, for we cannot recuperate the first night of *Love for Love*. We know only the cast list, the place of performance, and that the play pleased. One may compare a twentieth-century work like Synge's *The Playboy of the Western World* for which information is immense, but what we can deduce about *Love for Love* can only be from what we know or guess about Congreve's theatre in general.

The place of performance was significant. What Peter Brook calls 'the empty space' is where the actor begins. The theatre in Lincoln's Inn Fields to which Betterton led his company was an indoor tennis court. It had been used before as a theatre. The first occasion was in the wake of the Stuart Restoration (1660) which re-established

---

[12] I am indebted for information on stage history to Avery (1951).

[13] *An Apology for his Life by Colley Cibber* (Everyman edn.) p. 104.

[14] For information on the actors' careers see Highfill (1973–93). All the major roles were in experienced hands except for the teenage Mrs. Boman as the ingenue Miss Prue, and Mrs. Ayliff, a singer for the company, who stepped into the part of Mrs. Foresight (replacing the first choice, Mrs. Verbruggen).

the public theatres after their closure by the regicide republic.[15] Thirty five years later the same kind of space was as appropriate for Congreve as it had been for the first generation of 'Restoration' comic playwrights. Technically Congreve was writing the same kind of play. What the play needed was merely an 'empty space' within an auditorium. There are only two imaginary locations – Valentine's lodging and Foresight's house. As far as staging is concerned, therefore, Love for Love is simple and little scenery, if any, was required. This was pragmatically useful for a company re-adapting a tennis court, but this simplicity has a larger signification. The use of moveable scenery behind a proscenium arch had been one of the major developments of the Restoration stage and the interplay between action on the thrust stage *within* the auditorium and spectacle *behind* the proscenium arch was a rich source both for emblematic language and for extending the dialectic between 'illusion' and 'reality' intrinsic in all theatre. Love for Love eschews this for a comparatively Spartan simplicity. There are no conventional painted scenes for any of the host of contemporary locations mentioned: Pall Mall or Covent Garden, the New Exchange or the World's End.

Love for Love concentrates the action merely within the empty space of a tennis court now designated as a location for theatre. It is closer, thus, in twentieth-century terms to Grotowski's 'poor theatre' than to today's spectacle of the Royal Opera House of Covent Garden. In practical terms the actors on the stage and the audience – a few hundreds – shared the same room.[16] Both areas were lit. Many of the actors and audience knew each other personally. Since this was comedy in an up to the minute contemporary setting there was no distinction in dress or manners between actor and audience. Indeed, in some respects, the auditorium itself, since it was lit, might serve the audience as another kind of theatre for self-display, for wit or horseplay in pit, box or gallery, or for social rendezvous and sexual assignation. We know from anecdotal evidence of other plays that the audience might add their own com-

---

[15] The playhouses were closed in 1642 'to appease and avert the wrath of God'. On 21 August 1660 the newly restored Charles II gave Thomas Killigrew and Sir William Davenant 'power and authority to erect two companies of players' and 'to purchase, build or erect, or hire at their charge, so they shall think fit, two houses or theatres'.

[16] Styan (1986) conjectures that the tennis court was 75 by 30 feet, the stage 34 by 20 feet, and the audience capacity about 400. In seventeenth-century London the location in Lincoln's Inn Fields placed the company at the centre of their potential audience. 'The city, the Inns of Court, and the middle part of the town ... were the most constant support of a theatre' (Cibber, ed. cit., p. 164).

ment to the dialogue and that, at times, physical or legal restraint was necessary to prevent them intruding upon the stage itself. But we do not know how Congreve's specific audience in 1695 behaved. What was constant and acute, however, was the lived intimacy between actor and audience in a manner and degree unknown in the post-Irving darkened auditorium of the London stage. Nineteenth-century convention was to separate audience and actor by the proscenium arch, and in the twentieth century the members of the migratory and unlocalised public are unknown to each other and to the actors.

To understand the 'intimate' theatre of the 'Restoration'[17] – to know what it was like to be inside the Lincoln's Inn Fields tennis court in 1695 – knowledge of the audience is as important as knowledge of the acting conventions. It is a vexed and vexing question to which a precise answer is not available. In one respect commercial theatre has always been a 'democratic' institution. Anyone who can afford the price can attend and sit where they please. That included in the Restoration period King Charles II and Mrs. Pepys's maid servant. The audience, therefore, was heterogeneous. On the other hand seats were expensive. Pepys paid a maid eighty shillings a year and the cheapest seat would have cost her a shilling. But since, presumably, servants might have board and lodging, tips and hand-me-down clothes, a servant on eighty shillings a year was not excluded by price. On the other hand, although the potential audience in London was comparatively large (perhaps half a million) yet, between 1682 and 1695 the metropolis could support only one theatre company. Congreve writes (satirically) in *Love for Love* that the life of a play was three nights, and we know that theatre managements might improvise from show to show what might be offered next day. The first run of *Love for Love* (which was a major success) was thirteen nights. Let us not pretend to a mathematical exactitude for which the evidence does not exist, but that audience represents perhaps two per cent of the population of London, and less than a quarter of a per cent of the inhabitants of England. Compare the audience figures for a modern television soap opera where one third of the people in Britain will view a popular episode on any one night.

It is reasonable to envisage the audience of *Love for Love* as com-

---

[17] The word 'Restoration' is ambiguous. Strictly it applies only to the restored Stuarts (1660–88), but is often extended to the Licensing Act of 1737, or even the whole comic tradition from Etherege and Wycherley through to Goldsmith and Sheridan. It is used here to describe a continuity of style. Since Congreve was politically a 'Whig' he was a supporter of the revolutionary settlement of 1688 which expelled the Stuarts (an event alluded to in the rejected Prologue).

prising a small (but open) group of regular play-goers, sup-
plemented by those who had gone for a special treat. Different
entertainments might well attract different audiences, and commercial managements are always seeking to attract new patrons. But
Love for Love was as much 'as you like it' for the theatre-going
public as you could get. If so, that public was marginal. The overwhelming majority of people in 1695 did not see the play performed.[18] It was either unavailable, or they were indifferent, or they
were hostile. That massive absence is as significant as those present.
Popular culture might offer, on the other hand, texts such as Foxe's
Book of Martyrs and Bunyan's *The Pilgrim's Progress* or *Crumbs
of Comfort* (mentioned in *Love for Love*, III.565); or, to remain
with performance art, compare the congregation in every parish
church or nonconformist chapel every Sunday. Many of the major
subjects of controversy in Restoration England in religion (or politics) are absent from Congreve's comedy, as are most of the daily
concerns of the workaday world. This absence is as important to
the historian of theatre as to the theoretised ideologist. 'The way of
the world' which Congreve claims to portray is, as he is ironically
aware, *not* the way of the world – or, as the joke runs in *Love for
Love,* only a metropolitan clique would name a place in Chelsea the
World's End.

This absence of almost everything of importance from the tennis
court in 1695 is, paradoxically, the bridge between theatrecraft and
ideology. For going to the theatre is a spectacular act of useless
expenditure – no different from playing tennis. The symbiosis
between audience and actors is that, for the duration of the 'play'
both are members of a leisure class. People do not make money in
Love for Love, they spend it on 'pleasure'.[19] The audience, for the
duration of the action, are likewise at leisure for pleasure. This is
imaginary 'semiotics', of course, since the actors work for a liveli-
hood and so did some, at least, of the audience. It is not a cultural

---

[18] These figures are problematical. Love (1980) estimated either 4,000 regular
theatre-goers a year or 40,000/50,000 if the audience were entirely made up of
those who went for an occasional treat. Peter Holland (1979) estimated an average
audience at 500 and concludes that 'a significant proportion of the wealthy population' saw the plays – which may indicate how few 'wealthy' people there were.
The putting back of performance time after 1700 from 3.00 P.M. to 5.00 P.M. may
indicate that theatre companies were seeking to enlarge their audience by drawing
more from the workaday world of the city. See also Hume and Scouten (1980) and
Love (1967).

[19] See the discussion between Bellmour and Vainlove which begins Congreve's *The
Old Bachelor* and which defines 'pleasure' as the 'business' of the wits, and the
Prologue to the revised *The Tempest* 30 April 1674: 'for your pleasure wholly ...
designed'.

signification, however, cunningly concealed. On the contrary nothing is more up front (if one may be permitted a sexual allusion) than the recognition that the play is play and thus has no use.

In this respect the advance in scholarly apprehension of Restoration stage practice from Holland (1979) to Styan (1986) provides a base for a theoretised explication of Congreve's theatre-craft. What we are concerned with is 'metatheatre' (which is, *mutatis mutandis*, what Lamb meant by 'Utopian' theatre). This theoretical interpretation has been prompted by the experience of our own contemporary stage. There are, for instance, obvious analogies to Congreve in Pirandello's disjunction between actor and character, or in Brecht's theory of 'alienation' which demands that the audience eschew empathy to become critically aware of the play. Thus, by what Brecht called 'gestus' the actor reveals from without the signification of character by emblematic action. But, in the twentieth century, metatheatre is reactive since the purpose is to disrupt the conventions of naturalism and, thus, the modern writer of metatheatre is in conflict with the overwhelming forces of empathetic realism. But, for Congreve, metatheatre *is* theatre. There was no alternative. The audience and actor are not engaged in 'the willing suspension of disbelief' (Coleridge's phrase) but in the collective enactment of recognisable fiction. In these circumstances to put out the house lights would be nonsensical. The actors would not be able to see to whom they were talking, and the audience would not be able to see each other.

There are three principal elements in the creation of the meta-theatre of *Love for Love*: the constant reminder that we are watching a play; the formal construction of stage 'character'; and the constant intertheatrical reference to the corpus of dramatic experience shared in common by an audience of regular theatre-goers. The first element is so intrinsic to Restoration theatrecraft that only rudimentary indications need to be sketched. *Love for Love* would begin with the lighting and raising of the stage chandeliers thus designating the 'empty space' of the platform stage by establishing it as *within* the room of the auditorium. *Behind* the stage the raising of the curtain (not lowered until the comedy was finished) revealed an illusionary painted world the other side of the proscenium arch. The Prologue (and Epilogue) mark the beginning (and end) of play-time by direct address by actor in costume but out of character. Lest we should grow impatient, in Act IV.618–9 Valentine reminds us 'The comedy draws toward an end ... let us think of leaving acting and be ourselves'. That is as much to the audience as to Angelica, and forms of direct address, in character, continue throughout the action. The constant use of aside is the self-evident example, but aside and conversation between the characters are part of a continuum since both were out front – like the platform stage. One might equally step out of character at an appropriate moment.

When Mrs. Frail enters (unchaperoned by a maid – compare Angelica with Jenny) her first words are 'Hey day! I shall get a fine reputation by coming to see fellows in a morning' (I.480–1). The lines acquire an additional meaning when spoken by Elizabeth Barry, notorious for her reputed sexual liaisons, especially with the debauchee the Earl of Rochester, and, like Mrs. Frail, without a husband. Likewise characters move physically in and out of the play world since entrances and exits are through the doors of the theatre itself (practical stage doors in the set are a later invention of naturalism), or, if need be, 'straight through' the set as at IV.130:

JEREMY
    Mr. Scandal is with him, sir; I'll knock at the door.

Goes to the scene, which opens and discovers VALENTINE
    upon a couch disorderly dressed, SCANDAL *by him*[20]

Characters, or musicians, sing and play to comment on the action from time to time; appropriate dance provides further extension (one would like to know whether it were a *horn*pipe that Ben's sailors danced!), and a formal dance choreography marks out and arranges the movements of many of the scenes (the love duet of Tattle and Miss Prue for instance). Indeed, given the shortage of rehearsal time in the Restoration theatre and the crowding of the repertory, it is a reasonable hypothesis that formal and hierarchical blocking of the scenes was as well practised as dance itself. But ultimately the most pervasive signifier that this is metatheatre is the plot. It is the agent which generates major comic scenes – the discovery that Mrs Frail and Tattle have mistakenly married each other, for instance – but also the constant guarantee that, except in play, nobody behaves like this. Leaving aside small matters like marrying the wrong person in disguise, even our heroine Angelica outside of a play would be out of her mind to bestow herself and a fortune on a young man who has got bastards by whores, wishes the children had been murdered and has squandered every penny he possesses. But in play young rakes reform and (unlike everyone else) choose love before money (but get money as well) and live happily

---

[20] Valentine's mad scenes, in which he claims to be 'Truth', raise the issue of stage illusion and its relation to reality to an epistemological level in their 'hall of mirrors' effect: Society protects itself against those who speak the Truth by claiming that they are mad; but Valentine lies when he says he is mad; but Valentine is a character in a fiction which relates to other fictions (Shakespeare's plays for instance).... The roots of this 'deconstructive' scepticism lie in Christian humanism where the Platonic belief that we live in a world of deceptive shadows joins with St. Paul's 'Now we see through a glass, darkly'. The way in which deceptive appearances and uncertain values permeate the play is explored by Hughes (1996).

ever after. These are components of a theatrical code, the rules of which are enjoyable in their own terms. As Wilde's Miss Prism observed in *The Importance of Being Earnest*, the good end happily, and the bad unhappily. 'That is what Fiction means.'

In this kind of play, therefore, the naturalistic (Stanislavskian) creation of character would be disruptive. These are stage roles. But the development of 'gender studies' as a form of ideological criticism now provides another of those nodes where theatrecraft and ideology come into relation. For 'gender studies' are concerned with the social construction of sexual identity (or what older criticism of Restoration comedy called 'manners') and the subject of *Love for Love* is self-evidently sex and society. The pleasure of leisure is sex, and the actor, in creating a role, is also creating a social identity. But if gender in society is socially constructed, characters in plays are theatrically constructed. Informed criticism cannot ignore the play world to jump to social ideology. Here, again, our ignorance of seventeenth-century theatre demands care. The way the actors performed *Love for Love* in 1695 can no more be revived than the audience – whereas for *The Playboy of the Western World* (which could be used here as a comparative 'control') we possess directorial instructions, specific discussion of technique, stage photographs, moving film of some of the actors, and an acting style handed down from one generation to the next. For *Love for Love* nothing of that kind of specificity remains and one must work from the kind of suggestions provided by engravings of scenes from other plays, manuals of social deportment, or generalised reminiscences of players and audience.

We know, however, that Congreve considered the making of stage character an art of 'design' (as he writes in the dedicatory epistle of *The Way of the World*), and that three elements went into the 'design'. In his letter to John Dennis 'Concerning Humour in Comedy' he defined those elements as 'Humour' which is 'from Nature' and 'shows us as we are'; 'Habit' which is 'from Custom' which 'shows us as we appear under a forcible Impression'; and 'Affectation' which is 'from Industry' and 'shows us what we would be under a Voluntary Disguise'. Since he was writing comedy, the prime aim of 'design' was to create characters who were 'ridiculous' not by nature but by affectation.

On the reasonable assumption that Congreve knew what he was about, this tripartite 'design' offers a substantial range to the actor. It does not prohibit 'naturalism' as one element in the composition of character. It socialises that naturalism within the conventions of artificial society and it invites the actor to seek laughter by the exaggeration of both nature and manners by choosing affectation. Since the 'design' is tripartite, to remain in any one part of the range would be false to the playwright's conception – either total naturalism or total affectation, for instance.

This had to be achieved in the closest proximity to the audience. As Gildon remarked in his *Life of Thomas Betterton* (1710), the best actors always speak 'in the same Tone on the Stage, as they would do in a Room, allowing for the Distance'[21] and, as *Love for Love* indicates, even a covert 'wink and a smile' could be immediately picked up (IV.46). Since the action is this close up the actor could achieve the greatest subtlety of tone and innuendo and great rapidity of delicately inflected speech. It is a reasonable guess that Congreve wrote his dialogue with the potentialities of a small acting space in mind; and, equally, subsequent increases in the size of auditoria and the withdrawal of the action behind a proscenium arch would make the play cruder, slower, pantomimic.

Although the norm of speech was as if 'in a Room', the manners of 'society' make that room a formal space. Costume is for the display of status, taste and sexuality: the head-dress of the ladies (Ben fears they may blow over in a storm), corset, sexually provocative corsage and long skirt; the full wigs of the men, hat, top coat and sword, high-heeled shoes: these accoutrements control and formalise movement and generate the panoply of social signs by which manners define role and through which genders and classes intercommunicate. The semiotics of dressing (and undressing – to reveal the naked ape) belong to the leisure classes.

This cannot be known precisely because its theatrical meaning was dependent on acts of recognition and discrimination by the audience. What exactly was 'in fashion' in the leisure classes in 1695? What was going out of fashion? What might be coming in? What did manners reveal about where you lived, your rank, your social mobility? In this respect the way a man removed his hat, or a lady handled her fan, is an essential part of the comic language and thus intrinsic in the actors' embodiment of character and gender.[22] The audience would recognise the 'manners' and also respond to the perversion of the manners, because the aim of the theatrecraft is to provoke laughter by 'ridicule'. There are analogies also between social deportment and dance, and, indeed, dance was a central social activity. The grouping of actors within the design of the plot may well be controlled by a kind of dance analogy which gives each of them the opportunity for the display of virtuosity and a place in an overall pattern.

The basic control is distinction between the sexes. The play works by the sexual interrelation between 'woman' (as in Valentine's perplexed categorisation) and what Mrs. Frail more sportively calls 'fellows'. The basic binary division then subdivides

---

[21] Powell (1984) pp. 90–1.

[22] *Spectator* 102 comically describes the use and etiquette of the fan in detail. It is as important a stage property in Restoration theatre as in the Noh theatre of Japan.

into a pattern of humours and affectations: among the women the natural sexuality of Miss Prue; the sexual predator in quest of a husband (Mrs. Frail); the sexually frustrated wife (Mrs. Foresight); the old woman past sexuality (the Nurse); the heroine. Among the men: the natural sexuality of Ben; the sexual predator (Tattle); the heavy and sexually frustrated father (Sir Sampson); the cuckolded husband who, like the Nurse, is past sexuality (Old Foresight); the hero. This kind of intricate patterning of characters is distinctive of Restoration comedy and was quite impossible in Shakespeare, for instance, simply because half the dance (the women) were not available in his theatre.[23] But for both sides – women and fellows – it is type casting. A character called 'Scandal' is controlled by his name; Tattle is in large measure 'fixed' by Scandal's description before his entrance (I.323ff.) 'A mender of reputations! Aye, just as he is a keeper of secrets ... he is a public professor of secrecy, and makes proclamation that he holds private intelligence. – He's here. *Enter* TATTLE'. It is the function of fathers to be heavy (otherwise hero and heroine would marry in Act One), husbands to be cuckolds (unless heroes!), young men to be spendthrifts. The triple 'design' of character (nature, manners, affectation) is subordinate always to their role in the comic 'dance'. Accordingly any breach of that decorum by character or plot would be theatrically significant to a high degree. A rejection of Valentine by Angelica in the fifth act, for instance, might carry major ideological meaning. But the characters in *Love for Love* keep to the rules.[24]

But those theatrical 'rules' ultimately cannot be recovered either. Whereas today the semiotics of this actual 'text' of a New Mermaid edition isolates the play (and a performance would be an isolated experience), in 1695, for actor and audience, the play was a fragment in a vast repertory of contemporary theatre (or plays of the

---

[23] The royal patent of 1662 states, 'Foreasmuch as ... the women's parts have been acted by men in the habits of women, at which some have taken offence ... we do ... permit and give leave that all the women's parts to be acted in either of the ... two companies from this time to come may be performed by women'. Women had previously acted in the security of domesticity, but an attempt to import French actresses for the public stage earlier in the century had proved unsuccessful.

[24] There was a long history of the construction of character types which were read as indicative of normative human behaviour, deriving from Aristotle and Theophrastus in classical antiquity through to La Bruyère (in France) and, in England, John Earle's *Microcosmographie* and Sir Thomas Overbury's *Characters*. Literate members of the audience, therefore, would contextualise stage characters in relation to these precedents, to current stage conventions, and to contemporary manners and morals. Any attempt (for instance by twentieth-century feminism) to read the play as providing direct access to ideological norms needs to take account of this interrelation between genre, conventions and real world practices.

previous generation – Shakespeare, for instance, brought up to date). The play is also part of the repertory of the actors. One of the significations of there being only one London company between 1682 and 1695 is that the entire repertory was played by a handful of actors (who hung on to prime roles on a career basis, and whose replacement in those roles might be a major theatrical event).

Thus the central core of the audience would know (like Pepys) some hundreds of plays in performance and would recall a cast in a multiplicity of roles. *Love for Love* is inundated with intertheatrical allusions beginning with the Prologue which alludes to Wycherley's *The Plain Dealer* as a foundational play and ending with an Epilogue referring to Thespis's 'cart'. Scandal casts Sir Sampson in the role of Caliban (IV.181); Valentine run mad plays Hamlet to Sir Sampson as the Ghost (IV.234); Mrs. Frail plays Dido to Ben's Aeneas (IV.346ff.) – Purcell's opera was first performed in 1689 – and the episode is then discussed by Mrs. Frail and Mrs. Foresight in terms of heroic tragedy. But this is only the tip of the iceberg. The metatheatricality of the play does not depend upon direct allusion but on context: the entire repertory and the history of the company. One would not need an allusion to Wycherley, for instance, to pick out the relationship between Miss Prue in *Love for Love* and Marjorie Pinchwife in *The Country Wife*. Both are types of the country Miss come to town; both are given scenes to display the character in which they learn to lie. As for cuckolds, wits, fops, old lechers. . . . But it is unnecessary to multiply examples. In some ways Restoration comedy is like modern situation comedy. The whole point is formulaic repetition and variation. But it is unlike situation comedy because it is also in symbiotic relation to an alternative theatrical form, tragedy, which has its own conventions concerning fathers, lovers, husbands, wives, sons and daughters who act differently, speak differently and come to different ends. The same actors play both kinds of role on the Restoration stage. There was, therefore, by 1695, an infinite network of theatrical cross reference covering some hundreds of new plays, plus revivals from the archaic theatre of Shakespeare, all focused upon one company, or two, playing in the metropolis. Perhaps the nearest modern analogy is Hollywood's recognition of itself.

What happened thereafter in the eighteenth century is that *Love for Love* itself entered the repertory; was canonised; rewritten; and finally overrun by what my Introduction of 1969 called 'Podsnappery'. The most influential of early eighteenth-century periodicals, *The Spectator* 189 recognised the play as 'one of the finest Comedies that ever appeared upon the *English* stage', and Giles Jacob's *Poetical Register* (1723), supporting *The Spectator*'s assessment, provides a useful resumé of audience reaction, describing *Love for Love* as a work with abundance of wit in it, and a great deal of fine and diverting Humour; the Characters are justly distinguish'd, and the Manners well mark'd. Some of the nicer Criticks find fault with the unravelling of the Plot, and the Conduct of *Angelica* in it: But in spite of Envy, this play must be allow'd to be one of the best of our modern Comedies.[25]

Canonical status was finally achieved at the time of the opening of the Goodman's Fields playhouse (1732–3). The theatre was decorated with a statue of George II over the pit attended by Peace, Liberty and Justice themselves flanked by Shakespeare, Dryden, Congreve and Betterton.

As a canonical play *Love for Love* moves, as it were, out of the realm of contemporary applicability and criticism and becomes a status product to which audiences are attracted by star performers in familiar roles. Thus Wilks was to succeed Betterton as Valentine, Mrs. Oldfield replaced Mrs. Bracegirdle as Angelica, Colley Cibber took over from Dogget as Ben (and so on). Cibber's *Apology* indicates that it was the playing of Wilks against Oldfield in duels of sex and wit at this time which 'happily supported that Humour and Vivacity which is so peculiar to our *English* stage.'[26] The history of the play thereafter is rather the history of the actors who either held, or rejected, or shuffled the roles. The interchange between actor and society in the process remained as significant as in the theatre of the 1690s. One instance may serve for all and compress chronicle history into a significant emblem: Reynolds's great portrait of Mrs. Abington in the role of Miss Prue. The character, as Mrs. Abington portrays her through Reynolds, is utterly natural and sexually provocative (she is about to suck her thumb as she gazes enigmatically at the viewer – is she knowing or innocent, a mere child or a courtesan?). She is in the flower of youth, yet in the height of fashion. But the interchange between Mrs. Abington as actress and Miss Prue as character is as important as the image itself. She began as a flower-girl (like Eliza Doolittle) and became a prostitute. Socially floated off by a marriage to her music master (soon paid to keep his distance), she was educated by her lover, Edward Needham, M.P., and became a leader of fashion, the centre of a salon of the wits (even Dr. Johnson came) and the greatest comic actress of her time: 'in comedy, and above all when the manners of the first circles ... are to be parodied, she is unique on the English Stage'.[27] That she was eventually to be succeeded by Mrs. Jordan as Miss Prue indicates that the century is, in this respect, of a piece.

[25] Avery (1951) p. 5.
[26] Avery (1951) p. 37.
[27] Avery (1951) p. 115.

Mrs. Abington as Miss Prue in Congreve's 'Love for Love' by
Sir Joshua Reynolds, 1771. (With permission from the Yale
Center for British Art, Paul Mellon Collection.)

Mrs. Jordan came near the throne, for she was the mistress of the Duke of Clarence.

But Garrick's neglect of Congreve in the latter part of the eighteenth century coincided also with the gradual advance of the forces of moral correctness. The most important change in the history of *Love for Love* on the stage at this time is the shift in what was acceptable in the text. Congreve was progressively bowdlerised after 1776, although the process is not systematic or consistent. Scandal's railing speech (I.128ff.) was heavily blue-pencilled, as was the whole episode of the prostitute Margery. The unnatural teat in II.105ff. was also too embarrassing to stay in, and almost the whole of III.20–182 went. III.420–577 was radically cut including the entire wooing of Mrs. Foresight by Tattle. Oddly enough, although Ben's part was later pruned in the Act his song escaped (perhaps the bowdleriser was too innocent to work out the allusion in 'wind and water'). The song 'I tell thee, Charmian' went, however, as well as Angelica's 'She that marries a fool ...' (V.63ff.) and Sir Sampson's reply. The blue pencil was partly moral, but this is a long play which can readily carry cuts. The excisions became more severe in the nineteenth century, but by then the play was sinking with all hands.

The revival of interest in the twentieth century in part reflects the growth of scholarly interest in seventeenth-century theatre in performance in which William Poel and Montague Summers were influential.[28] It also reflects, partly, a change in moral climate for, after Ibsen's *Ghosts* (first performed in London in 1891) the verbal 'pox' of Restoration theatre is less likely to shock compared with the dementia of congenital syphilis. Nonetheless Restoration theatre was problematical material and re-emerged in the ambience of the Stage Society (1899) and subsequently the Phoenix Society (1919). The Stage Society was founded to produce plays of artistic merit which had little chance of performance in the commercial theatre. The sponsors were amateurs with professional standards using 'West End' casts in 'West End' theatres for revivals running for one, or two, performances, often on a Sunday night.

Under the auspices of the Stage Society *Love for Love* was revived at the Aldwych on the 15–16 April 1917 and by the Phoenix Society at the Lyric Theatre, Hammersmith on the 20–22 March 1921. The uncommercial nature of the Stage Society venture meant that there was little money for décor and that accordingly seventeenth-century theatre was explored on a bare stage (which is

---

[28] I have drawn extensively on the excellent accounts of Congreve on the modern stage in Morris (1972) and Thomas (1992). My own first-hand knowledge begins with the National Theatre production of 1965.

appropriate for *Love for Love*). Everything depended upon the actors. The scholarly drive behind the project also meant that early productions of the plays established a tradition of acting 'in period'. This has led to modern audiences taking it for granted that Restoration drama is 'costume drama'. If that seems self-evident, one need only compare the current alternative tradition with Shakespeare where the location of the stage action may be anywhere and the dress any time. Shakespeare, it seems, wrote universal myths in which every age finds its own ideological concerns, but Congreve wrote comedies of seventeenth-century 'manners'.

Perhaps. One of the consequences has been the emergence of what one might call the 'Nigel Playfair method'. Playfair grasped the essential point that Congreve wrote metatheatre, but metatheatre, for Playfair, meant an over the top gestural and toyshop theatre – actors stranded in cardboard cut-out attitudes, balletic servants lighting candles, stage quartets accompanying the action in costume, endless play with snuff, or lace handkerchiefs, a continual determination to be pretty, and, lest the audience grow bored, 'a rattling, jaunty, jigging, almost jazzing' style. This method has been immensely influential because immensely successful. Since there is no way to reinvent the precision of Restoration manners perhaps all that is left is a kind of parody, a comic English equivalent of Japanese Noh theatre where we laugh at the costumes and the fans, but no longer understand the real meaning of the language.

It required a great actor to transform apprehension of the potentialities of Congreve. Although Edith Evans's performance of Millamant in *The Way of the World* may seem paranthetical to the story of *Love for Love* on stage, it was her performance for Playfair in 1924 which revealed the power of 'character' in Congreve and comedy as tragedy seen from the other side. Playfair himself wrote 'What started as a comedy of manners [was] suddenly rapt from our sight in one of the most blinding visions of character that have ever been dramatized ... here is character rendered sublime by the poignancy and the sincerity of its wit', and Hubert Griffith, responding to the tragedy of the role, felt himself 'strangely moved' by 'an inward disturbance of spirit that neither wit nor gaiety nor the art born of perfect technique can produce'. It was a performance suspended between deep disillusionment and a hunger of the spirit to find love for love, and, technically a performance which combined the wit, thrust and poise of the contemporary theatre of Shaw with a Bradleyean sense of Shakespearean waste.

The success of the venture opened the door for the best talents of the theatre to spread their wings in Congreve. There have been four major revivals of *Love for Love* in the past half century: Tyrone Guthrie's in 1934, John Gielgud's in 1943 (following on his earlier production at the Oxford Playhouse) and Peter Wood's for the National Theatre in 1965, revived in 1985. Performance at the

National might be said to re-establish Congreve in the canonical
role he had first achieved by his incorporation in the pantheon of
Goodman's Fields in the 1730s.

Guthrie's production was distinguished by Charles Laughton in
the season in which he played Angelo, Henry VIII and Lopahin (in
Chekov's *The Cherry Orchard*). His Tattle was a *pièce de resistance*, 'a delicious figure of fun and under-breeding, a mixture of
wiggery and waggery, at once coy and servile, male yet mincing.'
His acting was seen as 'a form of total immersion, Tattle to the
writhing shoulders, the twisted mouth, the garrulous finger tips.'
But the playing as a whole achieved a sense of reality which surprised the critic of *The Times*. His view directly contradicts Lamb's:

> We have only to see a few scenes played to realise that, as readers,
> dazzled perhaps by the unending flicker of wit across the printed
> page, we have been led into a too easy acceptance of Lamb's theory
> that all these characters were intended to inhabit a world of fantasy.

Gielgud's version of 1943 was also a 'star' vehicle aiming at
verisimilitude. Gielgud played Valentine 'with a witty grace, a perfect command of the Congrevean prose rhythm and the nicest sense
of Shakespearean parody in the mad scene'. But it was Miles
Malleson as Foresight who stole the show, 'authentic' in his 'ago-
nies', 'his little peering, anxious face ... a haggard question mark of
pallid and twitching perturbation.' Gielgud explained his directorial
intentions in *Stage Directions* (1963):

> We ... felt that if the actors would all play realistically – and were
> also stylish enough to wear their clothes and deport themselves with
> elegance – there was no reason why we might not play the play in a
> naturalistic style, with the 'fourth wall down' as it were. This was in
> direct opposition to anything I had ever seen, for, in Playfair's pro-
> ductions, the asides were delivered (as no doubt they were in the
> eighteenth century) directly to the audience, and there was no
> attempt at localization in the settings, which were merely drop scenes
> and wings, and served as a background (but not as a home) for the
> characters in the play.

From realism to 'socialist realism' was the next step in Peter
Wood's production in 1965. The aim was to show the material
reality behind the sex and marriage market. Money is the root of all
capitalist evil. The date of the production is half way between, on
the one hand, the socialist theatre of Shaw (and Ibsen as interpreted by Marxist feminism), and on the other the current institu-
tionalisation of ideological criticism in academic (particularly
Shakespearean) criticism (the 1890s for the 1990s). For Wood the
catalyst was Brecht (and the theatrical model the Berliner Ensemble)

who became stylistically linked with the seamier side of Hogarth. Far from being 'the hero', Valentine was an ageing sloven in a filthy lodging, and a deliberate untidiness and absence of what Gielgud called 'style' was imposed directorially upon the company. Ben (Colin Blakely with an Irish accent) was a sort of villainous bagman and Geraldine McEwan as Angelica had the kind of pallor which results either from too many late nights or some unmentionable disease. Robert Stephens, as Scandal, became a moralistic Iago unveiling his spleen at a corrupt world. The overall pace was slow; the comedy bleak midwinterly. The company toured to Communist Moscow.

Equally remarkable in this extraordinary and unforgettable production was the resistance of some of the 'stars' to directorial theatre. Of these Olivier (in some ways the last Victorian) was uncontrollable as Tattle – a Felliniesque fop in commedia dell'arte make up, grotesquely padded and more a parody of a cat than a man. The London *Evening News* report of Olivier doing his own thing in the Kremlin Theatre gets his limelight bravura exactly. In escaping from Miss Prue's bedroom hopelessly dishevelled he ran

> along a narrow wall balancing himself like a drunken tightrope walker. Coming to a wide gap, this uncertain tomcat paused, closed his eyes in silent prayer and jumped across. This would be funny in any language.

It brought the Communist house down. The performance also shows how, across the centuries, individual characters – Angelica, Ben, Foresight, Miss Prue, Tattle, Valentine for instance – have each attracted star performers. Thus, even in a politically correct Congreve, the irrepressible individuality of his roles turns ideology into a series of comic turns.[29]

Since the tension between theatrecraft and ideology has informed both the original and revised editions of the New Mermaid *Love for Love*, a few words in conclusion on the editor's own experiments with Restoration style. It has been possible in a noncommercial, university environment to test ideas in practice with talented, dedicated and non-star casts. The first experiment followed hard on the heels of Wood in looking for the social relevance of Congreve for

---

[29] The stylish Bristol Old Vic production by Adrian Noble (1979) played *Love for Love* 'straight' for the delight of the characterisation, as did Ian Judge's at Chichester, 1996. The most adventurous production I know since Wood's is John Harris's at Hampstead in 1995 which started by parodying 'Restoration' posing and ended in black clothes before a black set in a cool and sardonic climax. The actors had difficulty in adapting to this stylistic variety which seemed to be aimed at revealing the dark underbelly of the Restoration peacock.

Leslie Phillips as Sir Sampson Legend in the Chichester Festival
Theatre production, 1996 (photo: Donald Cooper © Photostage)

the 1960s. What the 1960s seemed to have in common with the 1690s was an anti-moralist sexual libertinism combined with a sense of 'swinging' fashion. A young cast went up-to-date in hot-pants, miniscule skirts, Julie Christie hairdos for the women, a 'Rolling Stones' look for the men. The air was sweet with the smell of cannabis. The production exploded with sexuality and an exhilarating sense of the 'beautiful people' expressing the sheer joy of being young and free from work. But if the production was 'natural, simple, affecting' (as Goldsmith wrote of Garrick) yet modern manners could not encompass seventeenth-century prose style. The actors faced the dilemma that if you moved in a modern manner you could not speak seventeenth-century prose, and if you spoke mannerly you could not move modernly.

Accordingly a decade later I approached *Love for Love* as an English equivalent for Noh. The space was a Georgian town hall about the size of the Lincoln's Inn Fields tennis court. We built a thrust stage and painted the backdrop. The hall even had practical doors each side of the proscenium arch. The actors performed in what passes nowadays as Restoration style and each was given the opportunity to star. In many ways Lamb was vindicated. The play became extraordinarily beautiful and remote – almost a collage of texture and colour. Any break into naturalism was accordingly immensely powerful (but to be carefully used). The flash from Sailor Ben's eyes when he rejected Mrs. Frail was electric and like a thunderclap. But the sexuality and vitality of the sixties production could not be found.

In an ideal world perhaps Congreve's demand of character that it should be natural, mannered and affected might be perfectly realised and in types of universal human nature. I did not have the skill to find it, but of one thing I remain convinced, that the way into this play-text is to be found in the interrelation between actor and character in that special space of magic realism called the stage.

Note on the Text

Love for Love was first printed by Jacob Tonson in 1695. The present text is based upon this first quarto (Q1), and the copy text is from the Bodleian Library (Vet A 3e 112). There were three further editions in the same year, only one of which was acknowledged as the second edition (Q2). The third edition is dated 1697 (Q3), and the fourth 1704 (Q4). Congreve made a few minor revisions in these. For the collected edition of the *Works*, 1710 (W1), the text, in common with that of all his other plays, was extensively revised, partly to improve the sense and the grammar, partly to prune the play of licentious expressions. Acts were divided into scenes in the French fashion (on the entry or exit of a character). Three further editions of the *Works* appeared in Congreve's lifetime. The edition of 1719 (W2) claimed to incorporate further revisions, but these, as far as *Love for Love* is concerned, are very slight.

The present text is modernised in spelling, and the punctuation is a normalised version of the original. I have tried to preserve Congreve's rhetorical patterns while clarifying the syntax, rather than punctuate strictly according to modern conventions. The apparatus contains only substantive variants; punctuation, variant spellings, and contractions have been omitted and variants in the wording of stage directions between the first four quartos and the *Works* are not recorded unless they directly affect the movements of the actor. I have permitted myself some unacknowledged normalisations.

ABBREVIATIONS

Abbreviated references to works cited in the Introduction are keyed to the Further Reading section which follows by surname, then date. Thus Avery (1951) refers to Avery, Emmett L., *Congreve's Plays on the Eighteenth-Century Stage*, New York, MLA, 1951.

In the text of *Love for Love* the following abbreviations are used:

Davis	Davis, Herbert, ed., *The Complete Plays of William Congreve*, Chicago, University of Chicago Press, 1967
Summers	Summers, Montague, ed., *The Complete Works of William Congreve*, London, The Nonesuch Press, 1923
OED	The *Oxford English Dictionary*
Q1	first quarto, 1695
Q2	second quarto, 1695 (the acknowledged 'second edition')
Q3	third quarto, 1697
Q4	fourth quarto, 1704
W1	Congreve's *Works*, 1710
W2	Congreve's *Works*, 1719
Ww	both editions of the *Works*, 1710 and 1719
s.d.	stage direction

FURTHER READING

The Restoration Stage

Avery, Emmett L., *Congreve's Plays on the Eighteenth-Century Stage*, New York, MLA, 1951

—, Scouten, Arthur H., and Van Lennep, William H., *The London Stage 1660–1800, Part One: 1660–1700*, Carbondale, Southern Illinois University Press, 1965

Boswell, Eleanor, *The Restoration Court Stage, 1660–1702*, London, Allen & Unwin, 1932

Brown, Laura, *English Dramatic Form, 1660–1760: An Essay in Generic History*, New Haven, Yale University Press, 1981

Highfill, Philip H., Jun. et al. (eds.), *A Biographical Dictionary of Actors, Actresses, Musicians, Dancers, Managers and Other Stage Personnel in London, 1660–1800*, 16 vols., Carbondale, Southern Illinois University Press, 1973–93

Holland, Peter, *The Ornament of Action: Text and Performance in Restoration Comedy*, Cambridge, Cambridge University Press, 1979

Hotson, Leslie, *The Commonwealth and Restoration Stage*, Cambridge, Mass., Harvard University Press, 1928

Hughes, Derek, *English Drama 1660–1700*, Oxford, Clarendon Press, 1996

Hume, Robert D., *The Development of English Drama in the Late Seventeenth Century*, Oxford, Clarendon Press, 1976

(ed.), *The London Theatre World, 1660–1800*, Carbondale, Southern Illinois University Press, 1980

The Rakish Stage: Studies in English Drama, 1660–1800, Carbondale, Southern Illinois University Press, 1983

and Scouten, Arthur H., 'Restoration Theatre and its Audiences, 1660–1776', *Yearbook of English Studies* 10 (1980), 45–69

Leacroft, Richard, *The Development of the Playhouse*, London, Eyre Methuen, 1973

Loftis, John, et al. (eds.), *The Revels History of Drama in English: 1660–1750*, London, Methuen, 1976

Love, Harold, 'The Myth of the Restoration Audience', *Komos* 1 (1967), 49–56

'Who were the Restoration Audience?', *Yearbook of English Studies* 10 (1980), 21–44

Mullin, Donald C., *The Development of the Playhouse*, Berkeley, University of California Press, 1970

Nicoll, Allardyce, *A History of English Drama, 1660–1900*, vol. 1,

Restoration   Drama,   1660–1700,   Cambridge,   Cambridge
   University Press, 4th edn., 1952
Powell,   Jocelyn,   *Restoration   Theatre   Production*,   London,
   Routledge & Kegan Paul, 1984
Southern, Richard, *Changeable Scenery*, London, Faber and Faber,
   1952
Styan, J. L., *Restoration Comedy in Performance*, Cambridge,
   Cambridge University Press, 1986
Summers, Montague, *The Restoration Theatre*, London, Kegan
   Paul, 1934
   The Playhouse of Pepys, London, Kegan Paul, 1935

A Chronology of Criticism

Lindsay, A., and Erskine-Hill, H. (eds.), *William Congreve: The
   Critical Heritage*, London, Routledge, 1989
Dobrée, Bonamy, *Restoration Comedy, 1660–1700*, London,
   Oxford University Press, 1924
Krutch, T. W., *Comedy and Conscience after the Restoration*, New
   York, Columbia University Press, 1961 (first published 1924)
Knights, L. C., 'Restoration Comedy', in *Explorations*, London,
   Chatto and Windus, 1946, pp. 131–49 (first published 1937)
Fujimura, Thomas H., *The Restoration Comedy of Wit*, Princeton,
   Princeton University Press, 1952
Holland, Norman N., *The First Modern Comedies*, Cambridge,
   Mass., Harvard University Press, 1959
Van Voris, W. H., *The Cultivated Stance: The Designs of
   Congreve's Plays*, Dublin, The Dolmen Press, 1965
Loftis, John (ed.), *Restoration Drama: Modern Essays in Criticism*,
   New York, Oxford University Press, 1966
Birdsall, Virginia Ogden, *Wild Civility: The English Comic Spirit
   on the Restoration Stage*, Bloomington, Indiana University Press,
   1970
Donaldson, Ian, *The World Upside Down: Comedy from Jonson to
   Fielding*, Oxford, Clarendon Press, 1970
Novak, Maximillian E., *William Congreve*, New York, Twayne,
   1971
Hawkins, Harriet H., *Likeness of Truth in Elizabethan and
   Restoration Drama*, Oxford, Clarendon Press, 1972
Morris, Brian (ed.), *William Congreve*, London, Ernest Benn, 1972
Love, Harold, *Congreve*, Oxford, Basil Blackwell, 1974
Hoffman, Arthur W., 'Allusions and Definitions of Themes in
   Congreve's *Love for Love*', in *The Author in his Work*, ed. Louis
   Martz and Aubrey L. Williams, New Haven, Yale University
   Press, 1978, pp. 283–96
Williams, Aubrey L., *An Approach to Congreve*, New Haven, Yale
   University Press, 1979

Bartlett, L., *William Congreve: A Reference Guide*, Boston, G. K. Hall, 1979

Thompson, James, 'Reading and Acting in *Love for Love*', *Essays on Literature* 7 (1980), 21–30

Lyons, Patrick (ed.), *Congreve: Comedies: A Casebook*, London, Macmillan, 1982

Novak, Maximillian, 'Foresight in the Stars and Scandal in London: Reading the Hieroglyphics in Congreve's *Love for Love*', in *Renaissance to Restoration*, ed. Robert Markley and Laurie Finke, Cleveland, Ohio University Press, 1984, pp. 180–206

Zimbardo, Rose A., *A Mirror to Nature: Transformations in Drama and Aesthetics 1660–1732*, Lexington, University of Kentucky Press, 1986

Burns, Edward, *Restoration Comedy: Crises of Desire and Identity*, Basingstoke, Macmillan, 1987

Markley, Robert, *Two Edg'd Weapons: Style and Ideology in the Comedies of Etherege, Wycherley, and Congreve*, Oxford, Clarendon Press, 1988

Peter, Julie Stone, *Congreve: The Drama and the Printed Word*, Stanford, Stanford University Press, 1990

Hughes, Derek, 'Restoration Theatre', in *Encyclopedia of Literature and Criticism*, ed. Coyle, Martin; Garside, Peter; Kelsall, Malcolm and Peck, John, London, Routledge, 1990, 424–35

Thomas, Donald, *William Congreve*, Basingstoke, Macmillan, 1992

Gill, Pat, *Interpreting Ladies: Women, Wit, and Morality in the Restoration Comedy of Manners*, Athens, Ga., Georgia University Press, 1994

Canfield, J. Douglas, and Payne, Deborah C., (eds.), *Cultural Readings in Restoration and Eighteenth-Century English Theatre*, Athens, Ga., Georgia University Press, 1995

LOVE for LOVE:

A

COMEDY.

Acted at the

THEATRE in *Little Lincolns-Inn Fields,*

BY

His Majesty's Servants.

Written by Mr. *CONGREVE.*

Nudus agris, nudus nummis paternis,
Insanire parat certa ratione modoque. Hor.

LONDON:

Printed for *Jacob Tonson,* at the *Judge's-Head,* near the
Inner-Temple-Gate in *Fleetstreet.* 1695.

Motto. Horace II *Sat.* iii 184 and 271 (reading *paret* not *parat*):
stripped of his lands and paternal wealth he prepares to go mad
by regular system and method

DEDICATION

To the Right Honourable Charles Earl of Dorset and
Middlesex, Lord Chamberlain of His Majesty's Household,
and Knight of the Most Noble Order of the Garter, &c.

MY LORD,

A young poet is liable to the same vanity and indiscretion   5
with a young lover; and the great man that smiles upon one,
and the fine woman that looks kindly upon t'other, are each
of 'em in danger of having the favour published with the first
opportunity.

But there may be a different motive, which will a little dis-   10
tinguish the offenders. For though one should have a vanity in
ruining another's reputation, yet the other may only have an
ambition to advance his own. And I beg leave, my Lord, that
I may plead the latter, both as the cause and excuse of this
dedication.   15

Whoever is king, is also the father of his country; and as
nobody can dispute your Lordship's monarchy in poetry, so
all that are concerned ought to acknowledge your universal
patronage: and it is only presuming on the privilege of a loyal
subject that I have ventured to make this my address of   20
thanks to your Lordship; which, at the same time, includes a
prayer for your protection.

I am not ignorant of the common form of poetical dedica-
tions, which are generally made up of panegyrics, where the
authors endeavour to distinguish their patrons, by the shining   25
characters they give them, above other men. But that, my
Lord, is not my business at this time, nor is your Lordship
now to be distinguished. I am contented with the honour I do
myself in this epistle, without the vanity of attempting to add
to, or explain, your Lordship's character.   30

I confess it is not without some struggling that I behave
myself in this case as I ought: for it is very hard to be pleased
with a subject, and yet forbear it. But I choose rather to

1–2 *Charles ... Middlesex* (1638–1706). As Lord Chamberlain he was instru-
    mental in the licensing of the Lincoln's Inn Fields theatre which opened with this
    play. He was a noted patron of the arts.
6 *that smiles* (who smiles Ww)
7 *that looks* (who looks Ww)
7–8 *are each of* (are both of Ww)

follow Pliny's precept than his example, when in his panegyric
to the Emperor Trajan, he says, 35

> Nec minus considerabo quid aures ejus pati possint,
> Quam quid virtutibus debeatur.

I hope I may be excused the pedantry of a quotation when
it is so justly applied. Here are some lines in the print (and
which your Lordship read before this play was acted) that 40
were omitted on the stage; and particularly one whole scene
in the third act, which not only helps the design forward with
less precipitation, but also heightens the ridiculous character
of Foresight, which indeed seems to be maimed without it.
But I found myself in great danger of a long play, and was 45
glad to help it where I could. Though notwithstanding my
care, and the kind reception it had from the town, I could
heartily wish it yet shorter: but the number of different characters represented in it would have been too much crowded in
less room. 50
This reflection on prolixity (a fault for which scarce any one
beauty will atone) warns me not to be tedious now and detain
your Lordship any longer with the trifles of,

MY LORD,
Your Lordship's 55
Most Obedient
and Most Humble
Servant,
WILL. CONGREVE

36–7 *Nec minus ... debeatur* Pliny the younger, *Panegyricus* 3.2 (to the emperor
    Trajan) 'while paying due tribute to his merits, I shall remind myself of what his
    ears can endure to hear.'
41–2 *scene in the third act* perhaps III.451–509 (III.xi Ww)
59 *WILL.* (William Ww)

A
PROLOGUE
FOR

The opening of the new Play-House, proposed to be spoken by
Mrs. Bracegirdle in man's clothes.

Sent from an unknown hand.

Custom, which everywhere bears mighty sway,
Brings me to act the orator today:
But women, you will say, are ill at speeches –
'Tis true, and therefore I appear in breeches:
Not for example to you City-wives;   5
That by prescription's settled for your lives.
Was it for gain the husband first consented?
O yes, their gains are mightily augmented:
      Making horns with her hands over her head
And yet, methinks, it must have cost some strife:
A passive husband, and an active wife!   10
'Tis awkward, very awkward, by my life.
But to my speech – assemblies of all nations
Still are supposed to open with orations:
Mine shall begin, to show our obligations.
To you, our benefactors, lowly bowing,   15
Whose favours have prevented our undoing;
A long Egyptian bondage we endured,
Till freedom by your justice we procured:
Our taskmasters were grown such very Jews,
We must at length have played in wooden shoes,   20
Had not your bounty taught us to refuse.
Freedom's of English growth, I think, alone;
What for lost English freedom can atone?
A free-born player loathes to be compelled;
Our rulers tyrannized, and we rebelled.   25
Freedom! the wise man's wish, the poor man's wealth;
Which you, and I, and most of us enjoy by stealth;
The soul of pleasure, and the sweet of life,
The woman's charter, widow, maid, or wife,

Prologue this prologue is om. in Ww

  25 *Our rulers tyrannized* a political allusion to the Whig revolutionaries of 1688/9
     who resisted James II as a 'tyrant' and brought in William III. 'Charter' (29)
     alludes to Magna Carta as a safeguard of English 'freedom'. Avery (1951) notes
     that William III attended the first night of the play (p. 30).

This they'd have cancelled, and thence grew the strife.   30
But you perhaps would have me here confess
How we obtained the favour – can't you guess?
Why then I'll tell you (for I hate a lie),
By brib'ry, arrant brib'ry, let me die:
I was their agent, but by Jove I swear   35
No honourable member had a share,
Though young and able members bid me fair:
I chose a wiser way to make you willing,
Which has not cost the house a single shilling;
Now you suspect at least I went a-billing.   40
You see I'm young, and to that air of youth,
Some will add beauty, and a little truth;
These pow'rful charms, improved by pow'rful arts,
Prevailed to captivate your opening hearts.
Thus furnished, I preferred my poor petition,   45
And bribed ye to commiserate our condition:
I laughed, and sighed, and sung, and leered upon ye;
With roguish loving looks, and that way won ye:
The young men kissed me, and the old I kissed,
And luringly I led them as I list.   50
The ladies in mere pity took our parts,
Pity's the darling passion of their hearts.
Thus bribing, or thus bribed, fear no disgraces:
For thus you may take bribes, and keep your places.

36 *member* member of parliament/penis

PROLOGUE

Spoken at the opening of the New House,
By Mr. Betterton

The husbandman in vain renews his toil,
To cultivate each year a hungry soil;
And fondly hopes for rich and generous fruit,
When what should feed the tree, devours the root:
Th'unladen boughs, he sees, bode certain dearth,   5
Unless transplanted to more kindly earth.
So, the poor husbands of the stage, who found
Their labours lost upon the ungrateful ground,
This last and only remedy have proved;
And hope new fruit from ancient stocks removed.   10
Well may they hope, when you so kindly aid,
And plant a soil which you so rich have made.
As Nature gave the world to man's first age,
So from your bounty we receive this stage;
The freedom man was born to, you've restored,   15
And to our world such plenty you afford,
It seems like Eden, fruitful of its own accord.
But since in Paradise frail flesh gave way,
And when but two were made, both went astray;
Forbear your wonder, and the fault forgive,   20
If in our larger family we grieve
One falling Adam, and one tempted Eve;
We who remain would gratefully repay
What our endeavours can, and bring this day,
The first-fruit offering of a virgin play.   25
We hope there's something that may please each taste,
And though of homely fare we make the feast,
Yet you will find variety at least.

---

8 *upon the* (upon Ww)

12 *And plant* (well plant Ww)

14 *bounty* to support the new theatre 'many people of quality came into a voluntary subscription of twenty, and some of forty guineas, a-piece', *An Apology for his Life by Colley Cibber*, Everyman edn. p. 102

22 *Adam ... Eve* Joseph Williams and Susanna Mountfort had seceded from Lincoln's Inn Fields to the rival company.

25 *first-fruit offering* 'The fruits first gathered in a season ... with reference to the custom of making offerings of these to God, or the gods' *OED*

There's humour, which for cheerful friends we got,
And for the thinking party there's a plot.   30
We've something too, to gratify ill nature
(If there be any here) and that is Satire –
Though Satire scarce dares grin, 'tis grown so mild;
Or only shows its teeth, as if it smiled.
As asses thistles, poets mumble wit,   35
And dare not bite, for fear of being bit.
They hold their pens, as swords are held by fools,
And are afraid to use their own edge-tools.
Since the *Plain Dealer*'s scenes of manly rage,
Not one has dared to lash this crying age.   40
This time the poet owns the bold essay,
Yet hopes there's no ill manners in his play:
And he declares by me, he has designed
Affront to none, but frankly speaks his mind.
And should th'ensuing scenes not chance to hit,   45
He offers but this one excuse: 'twas writ
Before your late encouragement of wit.

35 *mumble* chew with toothless gums, see V.134
39 *Plain Dealer's ... rage* Wycherley's play (1676). The misanthropic hero is called
   Manly.

[DRAMATIS PERSONAE]

Men

SIR SAMPSON LEGEND, father to Valentine and Ben	*Mr. Underhill*
VALENTINE, fallen under his father's displeasure by his expensive way of living, in love with Angelica	*Mr. Betterton*
SCANDAL, his friend, a free speaker	*Mr. Smith*
TATTLE, a half-witted beau, vain of his amours, yet valuing himself for secrecy	*Mr. Boman*
BEN, Sir Sampson's younger son, half home-bred, and half sea-bred, designed to marry Miss Prue	*Mr. Dogget*
FORESIGHT, an illiterate old fellow, peevish and positive, superstitious, and pretending to understand astrology, palmistry, physiognomy, omens, dreams, etc., uncle to Angelica	*Mr. Sandford*
JEREMY, servant to Valentine	*Mr. Bowen*
TRAPLAND, a scrivener	*Mr. Trefusis*
BUCKRAM, a lawyer	*Mr. Freeman*

Women

ANGELICA, niece to Foresight, of a considerable fortune in her own hands	*Mrs. Bracegirdle*
MRS. FORESIGHT, second wife to Foresight	*Mrs. Boman*
MRS. FRAIL, sister to Mrs. Foresight, a woman of the town	*Mrs. Barry*
MISS PRUE, daughter to Foresight by a former wife, a silly, awkward, country girl	*Mrs. Ayliff*
NURSE, to Miss [Prue]	*Mrs. Leigh*
JENNY, maid to Angelica	*Mrs. Lawson*

A STEWARD, OFFICERS, SAILORS, AND SEVERAL SERVANTS

[The Scene: *in London*]

Men ed. (Men by Q1)
Women ed. (Women by Q1)
maid to Angelica (om. Ww)

LOVE FOR LOVE

Act I

VALENTINE *in his chamber, reading.* JEREMY *waiting.*
Several books upon the table

VALENTINE
Jeremy.

JEREMY
Sir.

VALENTINE
Here, take away. I'll walk a turn and digest what I have
read.

JEREMY (*Aside, and taking away the books*)
You'll grow devilish fat upon this paper diet.   5

VALENTINE
And d'ye hear, go you to breakfast. There's a page doubled
down in Epictetus that is a feast for an emperor.

JEREMY
Was Epictetus a real cook, or did he only write receipts?

VALENTINE
Read, read, sirrah, and refine your appetite; learn to live
upon instruction; feast your mind, and mortify your flesh;   10
read, and take your nourishment in at your eyes; shut up
your mouth, and chew the cud of understanding. So
Epictetus advises.

JEREMY
O Lord! I have heard much of him when I waited upon a
gentleman at Cambridge. Pray, what was that Epictetus?   15

VALENTINE
A very rich man – not worth a groat.

JEREMY
Humph, and so he has made a very fine feast, where there
is nothing to be eaten.

---

7 *Epictetus* (c. A.D. 55–135) a Stoic philosopher. He taught that we should be
  indifferent to sickness, pain and death for happiness does not depend on exter-
  nal things, and all things happen through Divine Providence.
8 *receipts* recipes

VALENTINE

Yes.

JEREMY

Sir, you're a gentleman, and probably understand this fine   20
feeding; but if you please, I had rather be at board-wages.
Does your Epictetus, or your Seneca here, or any of these
poor rich rogues, teach you how to pay your debts without
money? Will they shut up the mouths of your creditors?
Will Plato be bail for you? Or Diogenes, because he under-   25
stands confinement and lived in a tub, go to prison for you?
S'life, sir, what do you mean, to mew yourself up here with
three or four musty books in commendation of starving and
poverty?

VALENTINE

Why, sirrah, I have no money, you know it; and therefore   30
resolve to rail at all that have: and in that I but follow the
examples of the wisest and wittiest men in all ages, these
poets and philosophers whom you naturally hate, for just
such another reason: because they abound in sense, and you
are a fool.   35

JEREMY

Aye, sir, I am a fool, I know it; and yet, heaven help me, I'm
poor enough to be a wit. But I was always a fool when I
told you what your expenses would bring you to; your
coaches and your liveries; your treats and your balls; your
being in love with a lady that did not care a farthing for you   40
in your prosperity; and keeping company with wits that
cared for nothing but your prosperity; and now when you
are poor, hate you as much as they do one another.

VALENTINE

Well, and now I am poor, I have an opportunity to be
revenged on 'em all; I'll pursue Angelica with more love   45
than ever, and appear more notoriously her admirer in this

---

21 *board-wages* wages allowed to servants to keep themselves in food
22 *Seneca* (c. 5 B.C.–A.D. 65) a Stoic philosopher and tutor of Nero. He wrote on
   the virtues of retirement, and was immensely rich. He committed suicide on the
   orders of the emperor.
25 *Plato* (c. 429–347 B.C.) taught that the virtuous man is happy, the vicious
   unhappy. His teaching is the basis of the argument of II.305f: the human soul
   has three parts, the natural appetites, the spirit of resolution by which we may
   resist appetite, and reason that determines when we should resist.
   Diogenes (c. 400–325 B.C.) taught that happiness is obtained by satisfying only
   natural needs in the simplest manner. He was reputed to live in a tub whence he
   reviled the rich.
32 *men in all ages, these poets and* (om. Ww)

restraint, than when I openly rivalled the rich fops that
made court to her; so shall my poverty be a mortification to
her pride and, perhaps, make her compassionate that love
which has principally reduced me to this lowness of for-   50
tune. And for the wits, I'm sure I'm in a condition to be
even with them.

JEREMY
Nay, your condition is pretty even with theirs, that's the
truth on't.

VALENTINE
I'll take some of their trade out of their hands.   55

JEREMY
Now heaven of mercy continue the tax upon paper; you
don't mean to write!

VALENTINE
Yes, I do; I'll write a play.

JEREMY
Hem! Sir, if you please to give me a small certificate of three
lines – only to certify those whom it may concern: that the   60
bearer hereof, Jeremy Fetch by name, has for the space of
seven years truly and faithfully served Valentine Legend
Esq.; and that he is not now turned away for any misde-
meanour; but does voluntarily dismiss his master from any
future authority over him –   65

VALENTINE
No, sirrah, you shall live with me still.

JEREMY
Sir, it's impossible – I may die with you, starve with you, or
be damned with your works; but to live even three days, the
life of a play, I no more expect it than to be canonized for
a Muse after my decease.   70

VALENTINE
You are witty, you rogue! I shall want your help. I'll have
you learn to make couplets, to tag the ends of acts, d'ye
hear, get the maids to Crambo in an evening, and learn the
knack of rhyming. You may arrive at the height of a song,
sent by an unknown hand, or a chocolate-house lampoon.   75

JEREMY
But, sir, is this the way to recover your father's favour?

---

49 *that love* (the love Q3, 4, Ww)
51 *I'm sure I'm* (I'm sure I am Ww)
68–9 *three days ... play* the third night's proceeds were for the 'benefit' of the
   author
73 *Crambo* 'a game in which a player gives a word or line of verse to which each of
   the others has to find a rime' OED

Why, Sir Sampson will be irreconcilable. If your younger
brother should come from sea, he'd never look upon you
again. You're undone, sir; you're ruined; you won't have a
friend left in the world if you turn poet. Ah, pox confound   80
that Will's Coffee-House; it has ruined more young men
than the Royal Oak Lottery. Nothing thrives that belongs
to't. The man of the house would have been an alderman
by this time with half the trade if he had set up in the City.
For my part, I never sit at the door that I don't get double   85
the stomach that I do at a horse race. The air upon
Banstead Downs is nothing to it for a whetter; yet I never
see it, but the Spirit of Famine appears to me; sometimes
like a decayed porter, worn out with pimping and carrying
billet-doux and songs; not like other porters for hire, but   90
for the jest's sake; now like a thin chairman, melted down
to half his proportion with carrying a poet upon tick to visit
some great fortune; and his fare to be paid him like the
wages of sin, either at the day of marriage, or the day of
death.   95

VALENTINE
Very well, sir; can you proceed?

JEREMY
Sometimes like a bilked bookseller, with a meagre terrified
countenance, that looks as if he had written for himself, or
were resolved to turn author and bring the rest of his
brethren into the same condition. And lastly, in the form of   100
a worn-out punk, with verses in her hand, which her vanity
had preferred to settlements, without a whole tatter to her
tail, but as ragged as one of the Muses; or as if she were
carrying her linen to the paper-mill, to be converted into

81 *Will's Coffee-House* named after its proprietor William Unwin and located in
    Bow Street. Tom Brown describes it as the resort of four sorts of persons, 'beaux,
    and no wits … wits and no beaux … grave plodding politicians … and such as
    are both wits and beaux', *Amusements Serious and Comical*, ed. Arthur L.
    Hayward, London, Routledge, 1927, pp. 228–9. Congreve was a customer.
82 *Royal Oak Lottery* named after the oak tree in which Charles II hid after the
    battle of Worcester (1651). Ned Ward, *The London Spy* XV, gives an account
    of the lottery and the role of astrologers in predicting winning tickets.
87 *Banstead Downs* near Epsom. Pepys notes it as a popular venue for horse and
    foot races.
92 *upon tick* to obtain goods upon credit
94 *wages of sin* 'For the wages of sin is death; but the gift of God is eternal life'
    Romans 6.23
97 *bilked* to bilk someone is to evade payment of a debt
101 *punk* prostitute

folio books, of warning to all young maids not to prefer   105
poetry to good sense; or lying in the arms of a needy wit,
before the embraces of a wealthy fool.

Enter SCANDAL

SCANDAL
What, Jeremy holding forth?
VALENTINE
The rogue has (with all the wit he could muster up) been
declaiming against wit.   110
SCANDAL
Aye? Why then I'm afraid Jeremy has wit; for wherever it
is, it's always contriving its own ruin.
JEREMY
Why, so I have been telling my master, sir. Mr. Scandal, for
heaven's sake, sir, try if you can dissuade him from turning
poet.   115
SCANDAL
Poet! He shall turn soldier first, and rather depend upon the
outside of his head than the lining. Why, what the devil, has
not your poverty made you enemies enough? Must you
needs show your wit to get more?
JEREMY
Aye, more indeed; for who cares for anybody that has more   120
wit than himself?
SCANDAL
Jeremy speaks like an oracle. Don't you see how worthless
great men, and dull rich rogues, avoid a witty man of small
fortune? Why, he looks like a writ of enquiry into their
titles and estates; and seems commissioned by heaven to   125
seize the better half.
VALENTINE
Therefore I would rail in my writings and be revenged.
SCANDAL
Rail? At whom? The whole world? Impotent and vain!
Who would die a martyr to sense in a country where the
religion is folly? You may stand at bay for awhile; but when 130
the full cry is against you, you won't have fair play for your
life. If you can't be fairly run down by the hounds, you will
be treacherously shot by the huntsmen. No, turn pimp, flat-
terer, quack, lawyer, parson, be chaplain to an atheist, or
stallion to an old woman, anything but poet; a modern poet   135
is worse, more servile, timorous, and fawning, than any I
have named; without you could retrieve the ancient hon-

131 *you won't* (you shan't Ww)

ours of the name, recall the stage of Athens, and be allowed
the force of open honest satire.

VALENTINE

You are as inveterate against our poets as if your character   140
had been lately exposed upon the stage. Nay, I am not vio-
lently bent upon the trade. (*One knocks*) Jeremy, see who's
there.

Exit JEREMY

But tell me what you would have me do? What do the
world say of me, and my forced confinement?   145

SCANDAL

The world behaves itself as it used to do on such occasions;
some pity you, and condemn your father; others excuse
him, and blame you; only the ladies are merciful and wish
you well, since love and pleasurable expense have been
your greatest faults.   150

Enter JEREMY

VALENTINE

How now?

JEREMY

Nothing new, sir; I have despatched some half a dozen duns
with as much dexterity as a hungry judge does causes at
dinner time.

VALENTINE

What answer have you given 'em?   155

SCANDAL

Patience, I suppose, the old receipt.

JEREMY

No, faith, sir; I have put 'em off so long with patience and
forbearance and other fair words, that I was forced now to
tell 'em in plain downright English –

VALENTINE

What?   160

JEREMY

That they should be paid.

VALENTINE

When?

---

143 s.d. *Exit* JEREMY (JEREMY *goes to the door* Ww)
144 *What do* (What does Ww)
146 *used* (uses Ww)
150 s.d. *Enter* JEREMY (om. Ww)
152 *duns* debt collectors

JEREMY
Tomorrow.

VALENTINE
And how the devil do you mean to keep your word?

JEREMY
Keep it? Not at all; it has been so very much stretched that   165
I reckon it will break of course by tomorrow, and nobody
be surprised at the matter. (*Knocking*) Again! Sir, if you
don't like my negotiation, will you be pleased to answer
these yourself?

VALENTINE
See who they are.   170

Exit JEREMY

By this, Scandal, you may see what it is to be great;
Secretaries of State, Presidents of the Council, and generals
of an army lead just such a life as I do, have just such
crowds of visitants in a morning, all soliciting of past
promises; which are but a civiller sort of duns, that lay   175
claim to voluntary debts.

SCANDAL
And you, like a true great man, having engaged their atten-
dance, and promised more than ever you intend to perform,
are more perplexed to find evasions than you would be to
invent the honest means of keeping your word, and gratify-   180
ing your creditors.

VALENTINE
Scandal, learn to spare your friends, and do not provoke
your enemies; this liberty of your tongue will one day bring
a confinement on your body, my friend.

Enter JEREMY

JEREMY
O, sir, there's Trapland the scrivener, with two suspicious   185
fellows like lawful pads, that would knock a man down
with pocket-tipstaves – and there's your father's steward,
and the nurse with one of your children from Twitnam.

VALENTINE
Pox on her, could she find no other time to fling my sins in

---

178   *intend* (intended Ww)
185   *scrivener* one who supplied those who wanted to raise money on security
186   *lawful pads* not thieves (footpads) but bailiffs or constables
187   *tipstaves* officials carrying tipped staffs as a badge of office, i.e. a bailiff or con-
        stable
188   *Twitnam* Twickenham (west of London, and at that time in the country)

my face? Here, give her this (*Gives money*) and bid her   190
trouble me no more. [*To* SCANDAL] A thoughtless two-
handed whore, she knows my condition well enough and
might have overlaid the child a fortnight ago if she had had
any forecast in her.

SCANDAL
What, is it bouncing Margery and my godson?   195

JEREMY
Yes, sir.

SCANDAL
My blessing to the boy, with this token (*Gives money*) of
my love. And, d'ye hear, bid Margery put more flocks in
her bed, shift twice a week, and not work so hard, that she
may not smell so vigorously. – I shall take the air shortly.   200

VALENTINE
Scandal, don't spoil my boy's milk! [*To* JEREMY] Bid
Trapland come in.

> *Exit* JEREMY

If I can give that Cerberus a sop, I shall be at rest for one
day.

> *Enter* TRAPLAND *and* JEREMY

O Mr. Trapland! My old friend! Welcome. Jeremy, a chair   205
quickly; a bottle of sack and a toast – fly – a chair first.

TRAPLAND
A good morning to you, Mr. Valentine, and to you, Mr.
Scandal.

SCANDAL
The morning's a very good morning, if you don't spoil it.

VALENTINE
Come sit you down, you know his way.   210

TRAPLAND (*Sits*)
There is a debt, Mr. Valentine, of 1500 pounds of pretty
long standing –

193 *overlaid* smothered
195 *and my* (with my Ww)
198 *flocks* scraps of cloth used for stuffing
199 *shift* change clothing
203 *Cerberus* the dog who guarded the underworld in classical mythology. It was
   usual for the living who might visit the underworld to appease Cerberus with a
   gift of food – 'a sop'.
206 *sack* sherry

VALENTINE

I cannot talk about business with a thirsty palate. – Sirrah, the sack.

TRAPLAND

And I desire to know what course you have taken for the 215
payment?

VALENTINE

Faith and troth, I am heartily glad to see you, my service to you. [*To* JEREMY] Fill, fill, to honest Mr. Trapland, fuller.

TRAPLAND

Hold, sweetheart. This is not to our business – my service to you, Mr. Scandal. (*Drinks*) I have forborne as long – 220

VALENTINE

T'other glass, and then we'll talk. Fill, Jeremy.

TRAPLAND

No more, in truth. – I have forborne, I say –

VALENTINE [*To* JEREMY]

Sirrah, fill when I bid you. – And how does your handsome daughter? Come, a good husband to her! *Drinks*

TRAPLAND

Thank you. – I have been out of this money – 225

VALENTINE

Drink first. Scandal, why do you not drink? *They drink*

TRAPLAND

And in short, I can be put off no longer.

VALENTINE

I was much obliged to you for your supply: it did me signal service in my necessity. But you delight in doing good. – Scandal, drink to me, my friend Trapland's health. An hon- 230
ester man lives not, nor one more ready to serve his friend in distress, though I say it to his face. Come, fill each man his glass.

SCANDAL

What, I know Trapland has been a whoremaster and loves a wench still. You never knew a whoremaster that was not 235
an honest fellow.

TRAPLAND

Fie, Mr. Scandal, you never knew –

SCANDAL

What don't I know? – I know the buxom black widow in the Poultry – 800 pounds a year jointure, and 20,000 pounds in money. Ahah, old Trap! 240

---

239 *the Poultry* a street at the business end of London, east of Cheapside
    jointure property settled on a woman at marriage to be enjoyed after her hus-
    band's death

VALENTINE

Say you so, i'faith! Come, we'll remember the widow; I
know whereabouts you are: come, to the widow!

TRAPLAND

No more indeed.

VALENTINE

What, the widow's health; give it him – off with it! (*They
drink*) A lovely girl, i'faith, black sparkling eyes, soft pout-   245
ing ruby lips! Better sealing there than a bond for a million,
hah!

TRAPLAND

No, no, there's no such thing; we'd better mind our business – you're a wag.

VALENTINE

No, faith, we'll mind the widow's business. Fill again.   250
Pretty round heaving breasts, a Barbary shape, and a jut
with her bum would stir an anchorite; and the prettiest
foot! O, if a man could but fasten his eyes to her feet, as
they steal in and out, and play at Bo-peep under her petti-
coats, ah, Mr. Trapland?   255

TRAPLAND

Verily, give me a glass – you're a wag – and here's to the
widow.   *Drinks*

SCANDAL

He begins to chuckle; ply him close, or he'll relapse into a
dun.

Enter OFFICER

OFFICER

By your leave, gentlemen – Mr. Trapland, if we must do   260
our office, tell us. We have half a dozen gentlemen to arrest
in Pall Mall and Covent Garden; and if we don't make
haste the chairmen will be abroad and block up the chocolate-houses, and then our labour's lost.

---

251 *Barbary* Moorish; graceful in shape like an Arab steed
252 *anchorite* a religious recluse
262 *Pall Mall and Covent Garden* Pall Mall was a fashionable street north of St.
  James's Palace originally used for playing the game of 'pall mall' (in which a ball
  is driven by a mallet along an alley and through a ring). Covent Garden had been
  developed in the 1630s to designs by Inigo Jones, with a piazza of shops and
  apartments on two sides, with the gardens of Bedford House to the south and St.
  Paul's, Covent Garden, to the west. It was the fashionable social centre of 'the
  town'.

TRAPLAND
Udso, that's true. Mr. Valentine, I love mirth, but business   265
must be done. Are you ready to –

JEREMY
Sir, your father's steward says he comes to make proposals
concerning your debts.

VALENTINE
Bid him come in. Mr. Trapland, send away your officer,
you shall have an answer presently.   270

TRAPLAND
Mr. Snap, stay within call.

Exit OFFICER

Enter STEWARD *and whispers* VALENTINE

SCANDAL
Here's a dog now, a traitor in his wine. [*To* TRAPLAND]
Sirrah, refund the sack: Jeremy, fetch him some warm
water, or I'll rip up his stomach and go the shortest way to
his conscience.   275

TRAPLAND
Mr. Scandal, you are uncivil; I did not value your sack; but
you cannot expect it again when I have drank it.

SCANDAL
And how do you expect to have your money again when a
gentleman has spent it?

VALENTINE [*To* STEWARD]
You need say no more, I understand the conditions; they   280
are very hard, but my necessity is very pressing: I agree to
'em. Take Mr. Trapland with you, and let him draw the
writing. Mr. Trapland, you know this man; he shall satisfy
you.

TRAPLAND
Sincerely, I am loath to be thus pressing, but my necessity – 285

VALENTINE
No apology, good Mr. Scrivener; you shall be paid.

TRAPLAND
I hope you forgive me, my business requires –

Exeunt STEWARD, TRAPLAND *and* JEREMY

SCANDAL
He begs pardon like a hangman at an execution.

271 s.d. *Enter* STEWARD *and whispers* (*Enter* STEWARD *who whispers* Ww)
277 *drank* (drunk Ww)

VALENTINE

But I have got a reprieve.

SCANDAL

I am surprised; what, does your father relent?   290

VALENTINE

No; he has sent me the hardest conditions in the world: you
have heard of a booby brother of mine that was sent to sea
three years ago? This brother, my father hears, is landed;
whereupon he very affectionately sends me word, if I will
make a deed of conveyance of my right to his estate after   295
his death to my younger brother, he will immediately fur-
nish me with four thousand pound to pay my debts, and
make my fortune. This was once proposed before, and I
refused it; but the present impatience of my creditors for
their money, and my own impatience of confinement and   300
absence from Angelica, force me to consent.

SCANDAL

A very desperate demonstration of your love to Angelica;
and I think she has never given you any assurance of hers.

VALENTINE

You know her temper; she never gave me any great reason
either for hope or despair.   305

SCANDAL

Women of her airy temper, as they seldom think before
they act, so they rarely give us any light to guess at what
they mean: but you have little reason to believe that a
woman of this age, who has had an indifference for you in
your prosperity, will fall in love with your ill fortune;   310
besides, Angelica has a great fortune of her own; and great
fortunes either expect another great fortune, or a fool.

Enter JEREMY

JEREMY

More misfortunes, sir.

VALENTINE

What, another dun?

JEREMY

No, sir, but Mr. Tattle is come to wait upon you.   315

VALENTINE

Well, I can't help it, – you must bring him up; he knows I
don't go abroad.

Exit JEREMY

SCANDAL

Pox on him, I'll be gone.

VALENTINE

No, prithee stay: Tattle and you should never be asunder;

you are light and shadow, and show one another; he is per- 320
fectly thy reverse both in humour and understanding; and
as you set up for defamation, he is a mender of reputations.

SCANDAL

A mender of reputations! Aye, just as he is a keeper of
secrets, another virtue that he sets up for in the same
manner. For the rogue will speak aloud in the posture of a 325
whisper; and deny a woman's name, while he gives you the
marks of her person. He will forswear receiving a letter
from her, and at the same time show you her hand upon the
superscription; and yet perhaps he has counterfeited the
hand too; and sworn to a truth, but he hopes not to be 330
believed; and refuses the reputation of a lady's favour, as a
doctor says, no, to a bishopric, only that it may be granted
him. In short, he is a public professor of secrecy, and makes
proclamation that he holds private intelligence. – He's here.

Enter TATTLE

TATTLE

Valentine, good morrow; Scandal, I am yours – that is, 335
when you speak well of me.

SCANDAL

That is, when I am yours; for while I am my own, or anybody's else, that will never happen.

TATTLE

How inhuman!

VALENTINE

Why, Tattle, you need not be much concerned at anything 340
that he says: for to converse with Scandal is to play at
Losing Loadum; you must lose a good name to him before
you can win it for yourself.

TATTLE

But how barbarous that is, and how unfortunate for him,
that the world shall think the better of any person for his 345
calumniation! I thank heaven, it has always been a part of
my character to handle the reputation of others very tenderly.

SCANDAL

Aye, such rotten reputations as you have to deal with are to
be handled tenderly indeed. 350

328 *upon the* (in the Ww)
342 *Losing Loadum* a card game in which the aim was to lose tricks
347 *reputation* (reputations Ww)
347–8 *tenderly* (tenderly indeed Ww)

TATTLE

Nay, but why rotten? Why should you say rotten, when you know not the persons of whom you speak? How cruel that is!

SCANDAL

Not know 'em? Why, thou never hadst to do with anybody that did not stink to all the town.   355

TATTLE

Ha, ha, ha! Nay, now you make a jest of it indeed. For there is nothing more known than that nobody knows anything of that nature of me: as I hope to be saved, Valentine, I never exposed a woman since I knew what woman was.

VALENTINE

And yet you have conversed with several.   360

TATTLE

To be free with you, I have – I don't care if I own that. Nay, more (I'm going to say a bold word now), I never could meddle with a woman that had to do with anybody else.

SCANDAL

How!

VALENTINE

Nay, faith, I'm apt to believe him. – Except her husband,   365
Tattle.

TATTLE

O that –

SCANDAL

What think you of that noble commoner, Mrs. Drab?

TATTLE

Pooh, I know Madam Drab has made her brags in three or four places that I said this and that, and writ to her, and did   370
I know not what – but, upon my reputation, she did me wrong. – Well, well, that was malice, but I know the bottom of it. She was bribed to that by one that we all know – a man, too – only to bring me into disgrace with a certain woman of quality –   375

SCANDAL

Whom we all know.

TATTLE

No matter for that. – Yes, yes, everybody knows, no doubt on't, everybody knows my secrets. But I soon satisfied the lady of my innocence; for I told her – madam, says I, there are some persons who make it their business to tell stories,   380
and say this and that of one and t'other, and everything in the world; and, says I, if your Grace –

---

373 *one that we* (one we Ww)

SCANDAL
 Grace!
TATTLE
 O Lord, what have I said? My unlucky tongue!
VALENTINE
 Ha, ha, ha!   385
SCANDAL
 Why Tattle, thou hast more impudence than one can in
 reason expect: I shall have an esteem for thee. Well, and ha,
 ha, ha! well, go on, and what did you say to her Grace?
VALENTINE
 I confess this is something extraordinary.
TATTLE
 Not a word, as I hope to be saved, an arrant *lapsus linguae*   390
 – come, let's talk of something else.
VALENTINE
 Well, but how did you acquit yourself?
TATTLE
 Pooh, pooh, nothing at all, I only rallied with you. – A
 woman of ordinary rank was a little jealous of me, and I
 told her something or other, faith – I know not what –   395
 come, let's talk of something else.   *Hums a song*
SCANDAL
 Hang him, let him alone; he has a mind we should inquire.
TATTLE
 Valentine, I supped last night with your mistress, and her
 uncle old Foresight. I think your father lies at Foresight's?
VALENTINE
 Yes.   400
TATTLE
 Upon my soul, Angelica's a fine woman – and so is Mrs.
 Foresight, and her sister Mrs. Frail.
SCANDAL
 Yes, Mrs. Frail is a very fine woman; we all know her.
TATTLE
 O, that is not fair.
SCANDAL
 What?   405
TATTLE
 To tell.
SCANDAL
 To tell what? Why, what do you know of Mrs. Frail?
TATTLE
 Who, I? Upon honour I don't know whether she be man or

390 *lapsus linguae* slip of the tongue

woman but by the smoothness of her chin and roundness of
her lips.   410

SCANDAL
No!

TATTLE
No.

SCANDAL
She says otherwise.

TATTLE
Impossible!

SCANDAL
Yes, faith. Ask Valentine else.   415

TATTLE
Why then, as I hope to be saved, I believe a woman only
obliges a man to secrecy that she may have the pleasure of
telling herself.

SCANDAL
No doubt on't. Well, but has she done you wrong, or no?
You have had her? Ha?   420

TATTLE
Though I have more honour than to tell first, I have more
manners than to contradict what a lady has declared.

SCANDAL
Well, you own it?

TATTLE
I am strangely surprised! Yes, yes, I can't deny it, if she
taxes me with it.   425

SCANDAL
She'll be here by and by; she sees Valentine every morning.

TATTLE
How!

VALENTINE
She does me the favour – I mean of a visit sometimes. I did
not think she had granted more to anybody.

SCANDAL
Nor I, faith – but Tattle does not use to belie a lady; it is   430
contrary to his character. – How one may be deceived in a
woman, Valentine!

TATTLE
Nay, what do you mean, gentlemen?

SCANDAL
I'm resolved I'll ask her.

TATTLE
O barbarous! Why did you not tell me –   435

410 *lips* (hips Ww)

SCANDAL
No, you told us.
TATTLE
And bid me ask Valentine?
VALENTINE
What did I say? I hope you won't bring me to confess an
answer, when you never asked me the question.
TATTLE
But, gentlemen, this is the most inhuman proceeding –   440
VALENTINE
Nay, if you have known Scandal thus long, and cannot
avoid such a palpable decoy as this was, the ladies have a
fine time whose reputations are in your keeping.

Enter JEREMY

JEREMY
Sir, Mrs. Frail has sent to know if you are stirring.
VALENTINE
Show her up when she comes.   445

Exit JEREMY

TATTLE
I'll be gone.
VALENTINE
You'll meet her.
TATTLE
Have you not a back way?
VALENTINE
If there were, you have more discretion than to give Scandal
such an advantage; why, your running away will prove all   450
that he can tell her.
TATTLE
Scandal, you will not be so ungenerous. – O, I shall lose my
reputation of secrecy forever! I shall never be received but
upon public days, and my visits will never be admitted
beyond a drawing room: I shall never see a bedchamber   455
again, never be locked in a closet, nor run behind a screen,
or under a table; never be distinguished among the waiting-
women by the name of trusty Mr. Tattle more. – You will
not be so cruel!
VALENTINE
Scandal, have pity on him; he'll yield to any conditions.   460
TATTLE
Any, any terms.

448 *Have you* (Is there Ww)

SCANDAL
Come then, sacrifice half a dozen women of good repu-
tation to me presently. Come, where are you familiar? –
And see that they are women of quality, too, the first
quality.   465
TATTLE
'Tis very hard. Won't a baronet's lady pass?
SCANDAL
No, nothing under a Right Honourable.
TATTLE
O inhuman! You don't expect their names?
SCANDAL
No, their titles shall serve.
TATTLE
Alas, that's the same thing. Pray spare me their titles; I'll   470
describe their persons.
SCANDAL
Well, begin then; but take notice, if you are so ill a painter
that I cannot know the person by your picture of her, you
must be condemned, like other bad painters, to write the
name at the bottom.   475
TATTLE
Well, first then –

Enter MRS. FRAIL

O unfortunate! She's come already. Will you have patience
till another time – I'll double the number.
SCANDAL
Well, on that condition. Take heed you don't fail me.
MRS. FRAIL
Hey day! I shall get a fine reputation by coming to see fel- 480
lows in a morning. Scandal, you devil, are you here too? O,
Mr. Tattle, everything is safe with you we know.
SCANDAL
Tattle!
TATTLE
Mum. – O madam, you do me too much honour.
VALENTINE
Well, Lady Galloper, how does Angelica?   485
MRS. FRAIL
Angelica? Manners!
VALENTINE
What, you will allow an absent lover –

MRS. FRAIL

No, I'll allow a lover present with his mistress to be particular, but otherwise I think his passion ought to give place
to his manners.   490

VALENTINE

But what if he have more passion than manners?

MRS. FRAIL

Then let him marry and reform.

VALENTINE

Marriage indeed may qualify the fury of his passion, but it
very rarely mends a man's manners.

MRS. FRAIL

You are the most mistaken in the world; there is no crea-   495
ture perfectly civil but a husband. For in a little time he
grows only rude to his wife, and that is the highest good
breeding, for it begets his civility to other people. Well, I'll
tell you news; but I suppose you hear your brother
Benjamin is landed. And my brother Foresight's daughter is   500
come out of the country. I assure you, there's a match
talked of by the old people. Well, if he be but as great a sea-
beast as she is a land-monster, we shall have a most
amphibious breed. The progeny will be all otters; he has
been bred at sea, and she has never been out of the country.   505

VALENTINE

Pox take 'em, their conjunction bodes no good I'm sure.

MRS. FRAIL

Now you talk of conjunction, my brother Foresight has cast
both their nativities, and prognosticates an admiral and an
eminent justice of the peace to be the issue-male of their
two bodies. 'Tis the most superstitious old fool! He would   510
have persuaded me that this was an unlucky day and would
not let me come abroad: but I invented a dream and sent
him to Artimedorus for interpretation, and so stole out to
see you. Well, and what will you give me now? Come, I
must have something.   515

VALENTINE

Step into the next room – and I'll give you something.

SCANDAL

Aye, we'll all give you something.

491 *he have* (he has Ww)
506 *bodes no* Q1–2 (bodes me no Q3, 4, Ww)
507 *conjunction* the apparent proximity of two heavenly bodies
    has (hast Q1 uncorr. cited by Davis)
513 *Artimedorus* of Ephesus (2nd century A.D.), interpreter of dreams, palmist and
    author of *Oneirocritica*

MRS. FRAIL
  Well, what will you all give me?
VALENTINE
  Mine's a secret.
MRS. FRAIL
  I thought you would give me something that would be a   520
  trouble to you to keep.
VALENTINE
  And Scandal shall give you a good name.
MRS. FRAIL
  That's more than he has for himself. And what will you
  give me, Mr. Tattle?
TATTLE
  I? My soul, madam.   525
MRS. FRAIL
  Pooh, no, I thank you, I have enough to do to take care of
  my own. Well; but I'll come and see you one of these morn-
  ings: I hear you have a great many pictures.
TATTLE
  I have a pretty good collection at your service, some origi-
  nals.   530
SCANDAL
  Hang him, he has nothing but the *Seasons* and the *Twelve
  Caesars*, paltry copies; and the *Five Senses*, as ill rep-
  resented as they are in himself; and he himself is the only
  original you will see there.
MRS. FRAIL
  Aye, but I hear he has a closet of beauties.   535
SCANDAL
  Yes, all that have done him favours, if you will believe him.
MRS. FRAIL
  Aye, let me see those, Mr. Tattle.
TATTLE
  O, madam, those are sacred to love and contemplation. No
  man but the painter and myself was ever blest with the
  sight.   540
MRS. FRAIL
  Well, but a woman –

531–2 *Seasons* ... *Senses* popular prints. For the provenance and allegorical significations of the Seasons and Senses see Hall's *Dictionary of Symbols and Subjects
  in Art* (London, John Murray, 1974). The Twelve Caesars (after Titian) adorn
  the wall of plate III of Hogarth's *The Rake's Progress*.

TATTLE

Nor woman, till she consented to have her picture there too – for then she is obliged to keep the secret.

SCANDAL

No, no; come to me if you would see pictures.

MRS. FRAIL

You?   545

SCANDAL

Yes, faith, I can show you your own picture and most of your acquaintance to the life, and as like as at Kneller's.

MRS. FRAIL

O lying creature – Valentine, does not he lie? I can't believe a word he says.

VALENTINE

No, indeed, he speaks truth now: for as Tattle has pictures   550 of all that have granted him favours, he has the pictures of all that have refused him; if satires, descriptions, characters and lampoons are pictures.

SCANDAL

Yes, mine are most in black and white. And yet there are some set out in their true colours, both men and women. I   555 can show you pride, folly, affectation, wantonness, inconstancy, covetousness, dissimulation, malice and ignorance, all in one piece. Then I can show you lying, foppery, vanity, cowardice, bragging, lechery, impotence and ugliness in another piece; and yet one of these is a celebrated beauty   560 and t'other a professed beau. I have paintings too, some pleasant enough.

MRS. FRAIL

Come, let's hear 'em.

SCANDAL

Why, I have a beau in a bagnio, cupping for a complexion, and sweating for a shape.   565

MRS. FRAIL

So.

SCANDAL

Then I have a lady burning of brandy in a cellar with a hackney-coachman.

---

543 *she is* (she's Ww)

544 *you would* (you'd Ww)

547 *Kneller* Sir Godfrey Kneller (?1646/9–1723), the fashionable portrait painter, who painted the Kit-Cat Club portraits

564 *bagnio* bathing house (brothel)
         cupping being bled

567 *burning of brandy* (burning brandy Ww)

MRS. FRAIL
O devil! Well, but that story is not true.

SCANDAL
I have some hieroglyphics too; I have a lawyer with a hun-   570
dred hands, two heads, and but one face; a divine with two
faces, and one head; and I have a soldier with his brains in
his belly, and his heart where his head should be.

MRS. FRAIL
And no head?

SCANDAL
No head.   575

MRS. FRAIL
Pooh, this is all invention. Have you ne'er a poet?

SCANDAL
Yes, I have a poet weighing words and selling praise for
praise, and a critic picking his pocket. I have another large
piece too, representing a school, where there are huge-
proportioned critics, with long wigs, laced coats, Steinkirk   580
cravats, and terrible faces; with cat-calls in their hands, and
hornbooks about their necks. I have many more of this
kind, very well painted, as you shall see.

MRS. FRAIL
Well, I'll come, if it be only to disprove you.

Enter JEREMY

JEREMY
Sir, here's the steward again from your father.   585

VALENTINE
I'll come to him. – Will you give me leave? I'll wait on you
again presently.

MRS. FRAIL
No, I'll be gone. Come, who squires me to the Exchange? I
must call my sister Foresight there.

580–1 *Steinkirk cravats* a carelessly tied neckcloth (as worn by French officers at the
battle of Steinkirk, 1692)

581 *cat-calls* squeaking instruments used at the theatre to express disapproval

582 *hornbooks* first books for children consisting of a leaf of paper protected by a
leaf of transparent horn

584 *be only to* (be but to Ww)

588 *the Exchange* the 'New Exchange', shopping galleries on the south of the Strand.
'The chiefest Customers ... were *Beaus*, who I imagined, were Paying a double
price for *Linnen Gloves*, or *Sword-Knots*, to the Prettiest of the *Women*, that
they might go from thence and Boast among their Brother *Fops*, what Singular
Favours and great Encouragements they had received from the *Fair Lady* that
Sold 'em.' Ned Ward, *The London Spy* IX.

SCANDAL

I will; I have a mind to your sister. 590

MRS. FRAIL

Civil!

TATTLE

I will; because I have a tender for your ladyship.

MRS. FRAIL

That's somewhat the better reason, to my opinion.

SCANDAL

Well, if Tattle entertains you, I have the better opportunity
to engage your sister. 595

VALENTINE

Tell Angelica I am about making hard conditions to come
abroad and be at liberty to see her.

SCANDAL

I'll give an account of you, and your proceedings. If indiscretion be a sign of love, you are the most a lover of anybody that I know: you fancy that parting with your estate 600
will help you to your mistress. In my mind he is a thoughtless adventurer,

> Who hopes to purchase wealth, by selling land;
> Or win a mistress, with a losing hand.

Exeunt

---

592 *tender* (tendre W2)
596 *making* (to make Q4)

Act II

A room in FORESIGHT'S *house*

[*Enter*] FORESIGHT *and* SERVANT

FORESIGHT
  Hey day! What, are all the women of my family abroad? Is
  not my wife come home? Nor my sister, nor my daughter?
SERVANT
  No, sir.
FORESIGHT
  Mercy on us, what can be the meaning of it? Sure the moon
  is in all her fortitudes. Is my niece Angelica at home?   5
SERVANT
  Yes, sir.
FORESIGHT
  I believe you lie, sir.
SERVANT
  Sir?
FORESIGHT
  I say you lie, sir. It is impossible that anything should be as
  I would have it; for I was born, sir, when the Crab was   10
  ascending, and all my affairs go backward.
SERVANT
  I can't tell indeed, sir.
FORESIGHT
  No, I know you can't, sir: but I can tell, sir, and foretell, sir.

Enter NURSE

  Nurse, where's your young mistress?
NURSE
  Wee'st heart, I know not; they're none of 'em come home   15
  yet: poor child, I warrant she's fond o'seeing the town –
  marry, pray heaven they ha' given her any dinner. – Good
  lack-a-day, ha, ha, ha, O strange; I'll vow and swear now,
  ha, ha, ha, marry, and did you ever see the like!
FORESIGHT
  Why, how now, what's the matter?   20

  4–5 *moon ... fortitudes* the inconstant moon exerts her greatest power
 10 *the Crab* the fourth sign of the Zodiac. 'The sun being therein, goeth as it were
     backward (after the nature of the Crab)', W. Ramesey, *Astrologie Restored*
     (1660), II.xxiv – the source of much of Congreve's astrological lore (Davis).
 13 *tell, sir, and* (*tell and* Ww)
 15 *Wee'st* Woe is the

NURSE

 Pray heaven send your worship good luck, marry and amen
with all my heart, for you have put on one stocking with
the wrong side outward.

FORESIGHT

 Ha, how? Faith and troth, I'm glad of it! and so I have!
That may be good luck in troth, in troth it may, very good 25
luck: nay, I have had some omens; I got out of bed backwards too this morning, without premeditation; pretty
good that too; but then I stumbled coming down stairs, and
met a weasel; bad omens those: some bad, some good, our
lives are chequered, mirth and sorrow, want and plenty, 30
night and day, make up our time, but in troth I am pleased
at my stocking; very well pleased at my stocking. – O,
here's my niece!

     Enter ANGELICA

 [*To* SERVANT] Sirrah, go tell Sir Sampson Legend I'll wait
on him if he's at leisure. – 'Tis now three o'clock, a very 35
good hour for business; Mercury governs this hour.

           Exit SERVANT

ANGELICA

 Is not it a good hour for pleasure, too? Uncle, pray lend me
your coach; mine's out of order.

FORESIGHT

 What, would you be gadding too? Sure all females are mad
today. It is of evil portent and bodes mischief to the master 40
of a family. I remember an old prophecy written by
Messehalah the Arabian, and thus translated by a reverend
Buckinghamshire bard.

  When housewives all the house forsake,
  And leave good man to brew and bake,   45
  Withouten guile, then be it said,
  That house doth stond upon its head;
  And when the head is set in grond,
  Ne marl, if it be fruitful fond.

36 *Mercury* the god of merchandise and eloquence
42 *Messehalah* called by William Lilly, *England's Propheticall Merline* (1644) 'a
  learned Arabian'. Congreve possessed a copy of Lilly (see John C. Hodges, ed.,
  The Library of William Congreve, New York, New York Public Library, 1955,
  item no. 359) and drew most of the names of his astrologers thence. See III.439n.
43 *Buckinghamshire bard* John Mason (d. 1694), hymn writer and prophetic
  preacher of the second coming of Christ
48–9 *grond . . . fond* ground . . . found
49 *Ne marl* No wonder

Fruitful, the head fruitful, that bodes horns; the fruit of the   50
head is horns. – Dear niece, stay at home – for by the head
of the house is meant the husband; the prophecy needs no
explanation.

ANGELICA

Well, but I can neither make you a cuckold, uncle, by going
abroad; nor secure you from being one, by staying at home.   55

FORESIGHT

Yes, yes; while there's one woman left, the prophecy is not
in full force.

ANGELICA

But my inclinations are in force; I have a mind to go
abroad; and if you won't lend me your coach, I'll take a
hackney or a chair and leave you to erect a scheme and find   60
who's in conjunction with your wife. Why don't you keep
her at home, if you're jealous when she's abroad? You
know my aunt is a little retrograde (as you call it) in her
nature. Uncle, I'm afraid you are not lord of the ascendant,
ha, ha, ha!   65

FORESIGHT

Well, Jill-flirt, you are very pert, and always ridiculing that
celestial science.

ANGELICA

Nay, uncle, don't be angry. If you are, I'll reap up all your
false prophecies, ridiculous dreams and idle divinations. I'll
swear you are a nuisance to the neighbourhood. What a   70
bustle did you keep against the last invisible eclipse, laying
in provision, as 'twere for a siege? What a world of fire and
candle, matches and tinderboxes did you purchase! One
would have thought we were ever after to live under-
ground, or at least making a voyage to Greenland to   75
inhabit there all the dark season.

FORESIGHT

Why, you malapert slut –

58–64 *inclinations ... ascendant* sexual puns playing on 'inclination' in its astro-
    nomical sense, 'erect a scheme' (devise a horoscope) 'conjunction' (see I.506)
    'retrograde' (a planet is said to be retrograde when it appears to move backwards
    through the zodiac) 'ascendant' (the part of the zodiac on the eastern horizon
    at the time of birth was supposed to exert a commanding influence over one's
    life)
62 *jealous when* (jealous of her when Ww)
71 *last invisible eclipse* two eclipses of the sun during 1695 were given in the
    almanacs, but were 'not visible in London' (Davis)
77 *malapert* saucy

ANGELICA
Will you lend me your coach, or I'll go on – nay, I'll declare
how you prophesied Popery was coming, only because the
butler had mislaid some of the apostles' spoons and   80
thought they were lost. Away went religion and spoon-
meat together. Indeed, uncle, I'll indict you for a wizard.
FORESIGHT
How, hussy! was there ever such a provoking minx?
NURSE
O merciful father, how she talks!
ANGELICA
Yes, I can make oath of your unlawful midnight practices;   85
you and the old nurse there –
NURSE
Marry, heaven defend! I at midnight practices – O Lord,
what's here to do? I in unlawful doings with my master's
worship! Why, did you ever hear the like now? – Sir, did
ever I do anything of your midnight concerns – but warm   90
your bed, and tuck you up, and set the candle, and your
tobacco-box, and your urinal by you, and now and then
rub the soles of your feet? – O Lord, I!
ANGELICA
Yes, I saw you together, through the keyhole of the closet,
one night, like Saul and the Witch of Endor, turning the   95
sieve and shears, and pricking your thumbs, to write poor
innocent servants' names in blood, about a little nutmeg-
grater, which she had forgot in the caudle-cup. Nay, I know
something worse, if I would speak of it –
FORESIGHT
I defy you, hussy! But I'll remember this, I'll be revenged on   100
you, cockatrice; I'll hamper you. – You have your fortune
in your own hands, but I'll find a way to make your lover,
your prodigal spendthrift gallant, Valentine, pay for all, I
will.

79 *Popery was coming* an allusion to the supposed Roman Catholic plot ('the
   Popish Plot') of 1678 to murder Charles II, and place the Catholic James II on
   the throne
80 *apostles' spoons* spoons with figures of the apostles on the handles
95 *Witch of Endor* See I Samuel xxviii.
96 *sieve and shears* a form of divination. 'The Novice may as well believe,/The
   Scizars turning with the *Sive*,/As Pin their Faith on Conj'rers Dreams,/Of *Planets,*
   Houses and their Schemes.' Ned Ward, *The London Spy* XVIII.
98 *caudle-cup* thin gruel, mixed with wine or beer, spiced and sweetened
101 *cockatrice* a serpent, hatched from a cock's egg, which killed by its look

ANGELICA

Will you? I care not, but all shall out then. – Look to it,   105
nurse; I can bring witness that you have a great unnatural
teat under your left arm, and he another; and that you
suckle a young devil in the shape of a tabby-cat by turns; I
can.

NURSE

A teat, a teat, I an unnatural teat! O the false slanderous   110
thing! Feel, feel here, if I have anything but like another
Christian (*Crying*) or any teats but two that han't given
suck this thirty years.

FORESIGHT

I will have patience, since it is the will of the stars I should
be thus tormented. This is the effect of the malicious con-   115
junctions and oppositions in the third house of my nativity;
there the curse of kindred was foretold. – But I will have my
doors locked up – I'll punish you, not a man shall enter my
house.

ANGELICA

Do, uncle, lock 'em up quickly before my aunt come home.   120
You'll have a letter for alimony tomorrow morning. But let
me be gone first, and then let no mankind come near the
house, but converse with spirits and the celestial signs, the
Bull, and the Ram, and the Goat. Bless me! There are a
great many horned beasts among the twelve signs, uncle.   125
But cuckolds go to heaven.

FORESIGHT

But there's but one Virgin among the twelve signs, spitfire,
but one Virgin.

ANGELICA

Nor there had not been that one, if she had had to do with
anything but astrologers, uncle. That makes my aunt go   130
abroad.

FORESIGHT

How? How? Is that the reason? Come, you know something; tell me, and I'll forgive you; do, good niece. Come,
you shall have my coach and horses, faith and troth you
shall. Does my wife complain? Come, I know women tell   135
one another. She is young and sanguine, has a wanton hazel
eye, and was born under Gemini, which may incline her to

---

105 *to it* (to't Ww)
112–13 *or any teats ... years* (om. Ww)
116 *oppositions* the situation of heavenly bodies 180° apart
         third house the third division of the Zodiac relates to brethren

society; she has a mole upon her lip, with a moist palm, and
an open liberality on the mount of Venus.

ANGELICA

Ha, ha, ha!   140

FORESIGHT

Do you laugh? Well, gentlewoman, I'll – but come, be a
good girl, don't perplex your poor uncle, tell me – won't
you speak? Odd, I'll –

Enter SERVANT

SERVANT

Sir Sampson is coming down to wait upon you.

ANGELICA

Goodbye, uncle. [*To* SERVANT] Call me a chair. I'll find out   145
my aunt, and tell her she must not come home.

Exit ANGELICA *and* SERVANT

FORESIGHT

I'm so perplexed and vexed, I am not fit to receive him; I
shall scarce recover myself before the hour be past. Go,
nurse, tell Sir Sampson I'm ready to wait on him.

NURSE

Yes, sir.   *Exit*   150

FORESIGHT

Well – why if I was born to be a cuckold, there's no more
to be said –

Enter SIR SAMPSON LEGEND *with a paper*

SIR SAMPSON

Nor no more to be done, old boy; that's plain. – Here 'tis,
I have it in my hand, old Ptolemy; I'll make the ungracious
prodigal know who begat him; I will, old Nostrodamus.   155
What, I warrant my son thought nothing belonged to a
father but forgiveness and affection; no authority, no cor-
rection, no arbitrary power; nothing to be done, but for
him to offend, and me to pardon. I warrant you, if he
danced till doomsday, he thought I was to pay the piper. 160

138–9 *a mole ... Venus*. These were all signs of sensuality.
146 s.d. *Exit* ANGELICA *and* SERVANT (om. Ww)
150 s.d. *Exit* (om. Ww)
152 *said* – (said – he's here already. Ww)
154 *Ptolemy* of Alexandria (2nd century A.D.), astronomer who believed the earth
     was the centre of the universe
155 *Nostrodamus* (1503–66) French physician and astrologer. He published a book
     of rhymed prophecies, *Centuries*.

Well, but here it is under black and white, *signatum*, *sig-*
illatum, and *deliberatum*; that as soon as my son Benjamin
is arrived, he is to make over to him his right of inheritance.
Where's my daughter that is to be? – Hah! old Merlin!
Body o'me, I'm so glad I'm revenged on this undutiful   165
rogue.

FORESIGHT
Odso, let me see; let me see the paper. – Aye, faith and
troth, here 'tis, if it will but hold. I wish things were done
and the conveyance made. When was this signed, what
hour? Odso, you should have consulted me for the time.   170
Well, but we'll make haste –

SIR SAMPSON
Haste, aye, aye; haste enough. My son Ben will be in town
tonight. I have ordered my lawyer to draw up writings of
settlement and jointure. All shall be done tonight. No
matter for the time; prithee, brother Foresight, leave super-   175
stition. Pox o'th' time; there's no time but the time present,
there's no more to be said of what's past, and all that is to
come will happen. If the sun shine by day and the stars by
night, why, we shall know one another's faces without the
help of a candle, and that's all the stars are good for.   180

FORESIGHT
How, how? Sir Sampson, that all? Give me leave to contradict you, and tell you, you are ignorant.

SIR SAMPSON
I tell you I am wise; and *sapiens dominabitur astris*; there's
Latin for you to prove it, and an argument to confound
your Ephemeris. Ignorant! I tell you, I have travelled, old   185
Fircu, and know the globe. I have seen the Antipodes,
where the sun rises at midnight, and sets at noonday.

FORESIGHT
But I tell you, I have travelled, and travelled in the celestial
spheres, know the signs and the planets, and their houses;
can judge of motions direct and retrograde, of sextiles,   190

161–2 *signatum ... deliberatum* signed, sealed, decided
164 *Merlin* Alluding to the Arthurian magician's feats of divination, and, perhaps, to
the assistance he gave in the marriage of Uther and Igraine from which Arthur
was born.
183 *sapiens dominabitur astris* the wise man will be superior to the stars. The tag was
attributed to Ptolemy (Davis).
185 *Ephemeris* almanac
186 *Fircu* familiar spirit?
190–1 *sextiles ... oppositions* the aspect of two planets as seen from earth distant
from each other by a sixth, a quarter, a third or half the circle of the Zodiac

quadrates, trines and oppositions, fiery trigons and aquatical trigons; know whether life shall be long or short, happy
or unhappy, whether diseases are curable or incurable, if
journeys shall be prosperous, undertakings successful, or
goods stolen recovered, I know –   195

SIR SAMPSON
I know the length of the Emperor of China's foot, have
kissed the Great Mogul's slipper, and rid a-hunting upon an
elephant with the Cham of Tartary. Body o'me, I have
made a cuckold of a king, and the present Majesty of
Bantam is the issue of these loins.   200

FORESIGHT
I know when travellers lie or speak truth, when they don't
know it themselves.

SIR SAMPSON
I have known an astrologer made a cuckold in the twinkling of a star, and seen a conjurer that could not keep the
devil out of his wife's circle.   205

FORESIGHT (Aside)
What, does he twit me with my wife too? I must be better
informed of this. – Do you mean my wife, Sir Sampson?
Though you made a cuckold of the King of Bantam, yet by
the body of the sun –

SIR SAMPSON
By the horns of the moon, you would say, Brother   210
Capricorn.

FORESIGHT
Capricorn in your teeth, thou modern Mandeville;
Ferdinand Mendez Pinto was but a type of thee, thou liar
of the first magnitude. Take back your paper of inheritance;
send your son to sea again. I'll wed my daughter to an   215
Egyptian mummy, ere she shall incorporate with a contem-
ner of sciences and a defamer of virtue.

SIR SAMPSON
Body o'me, I have gone too far; I must not provoke honest

191–2 *fiery trigons and aquatical trigons* a trigon is the conjunction of three signs of
  the Zodiac; the fiery trigon: Aries, Leo, Sagittarius; the aquatical: Cancer,
  Scorpio, Pisces
200 *Bantam* in Java
205 *wife's* Ww (wives Qq)
211 *Capricorn* alluding to the Zodiacal sign 'the goat'; horns were the sign of a cuckold
212–13 *Mandeville ... Pinto* Sir John Mandeville the reputed author of a four-
  teenth-century travel guide to the Holy Land and the east; Fernão Mendes Pinto
  (?1509–83) author of *Peregrinação*, an account of his travels in the east

Albumazar. – An Egyptian mummy is an illustrious creature, my trusty hieroglyphic, and may have significations of   220
futurity about him; odsbud, I would my son were an
Egyptian mummy for thy sake. What, thou art not angry
for a jest, my good Haly? I reverence the sun, moon and
stars with all my heart. What, I'll make thee a present of a
mummy: now I think on't, body o'me, I have a shoulder of   225
an Egyptian king that I purloined from one of the pyramids,
powdered with hieroglyphics; thou shalt have it sent home
to thy house, and make an entertainment for all the philomaths and students in physic and astrology in and about
London.   230

FORESIGHT
But what do you know of my wife, Sir Sampson?

SIR SAMPSON
Thy wife is a constellation of virtues; she's the moon, and
thou art the man in the moon: nay, she is more illustrious
than the moon, for she has her chastity without her incon-   235
stancy. 'S'bud, I was but in jest.

Enter JEREMY

How now, who sent for you? Ha! what would you have?

FORESIGHT
Nay, if you were but in jest. – Who's that fellow? I don't
like his physiognomy.

SIR SAMPSON
My son, sir? What son, sir? My son Benjamin, hoh?

JEREMY
No, sir, Mr. Valentine, my master. 'Tis the first time he has   240
been abroad since his confinement, and he comes to pay his
duty to you.

SIR SAMPSON
Well, sir.

Enter VALENTINE

JEREMY
He is here, sir.

---

219 *Albumazar* an Arabian astrologer. Thomas Tomkis's play *Albumazar* (1615)
    had been revived in 1668.
223 *Haly* Referred to by Lilly as Hally Rodboan, and mentioned in Tomkis's
    Albumazar. Cited as an authority in predicting the weather in W. Ramesey,
    Astrologie Restored (1660) (Davis).
227 *sent home* (brought home Ww)
228–9 *philomaths* lovers of learning in mathematics (and astrology)

VALENTINE
Your blessing, sir.   245

SIR SAMPSON
You've had it already, sir: I think I sent it you today in a bill
of four thousand pound. A great deal of money, brother
Foresight.

FORESIGHT
Aye, indeed, Sir Sampson, a great deal of money for a
young man; I wonder what he can do with it!   250

SIR SAMPSON
Body o'me, so do I. – Hark ye, Valentine, if there is too
much, refund the superfluity; do'st hear, boy?

VALENTINE
Superfluity, sir; it will scarce pay my debts. I hope you will
have more indulgence than to oblige me to those hard conditions which my necessity signed to.   255

SIR SAMPSON
Sir, how; I beseech you, what were you pleased to intimate
concerning indulgence?

VALENTINE
Why, sir, that you would not go to the extremity of the conditions, but release me at least from some part.

SIR SAMPSON
O, sir, I understand you, – that's all, ha?   260

VALENTINE
Yes, sir, all that I presume to ask. – But what you, out of
fatherly fondness, will be pleased to add, shall be doubly
welcome.

SIR SAMPSON
No doubt of it, sweet sir, but your filial piety and my
fatherly fondness would fit like two tallies. – Here's a   265
rogue, brother Foresight, makes a bargain under hand and
seal in the morning, and would be released from it in the
afternoon. – Here's a rogue, dog, here's conscience and
honesty; this is your wit now, this is the morality of your
wits! You are a wit, and have been a beau, and may be a –   270
why, sirrah, is it not here under hand and seal? Can you
deny it?

VALENTINE
Sir, I don't deny it.

SIR SAMPSON
Sirrah, you'll be hanged; I shall live to see you go up

---

251 *is too* (be too Ww)

265 *like two tallies* Two halves of a stick were notched to represent the amount of a
     debt; matching the halves was proof of the debt.

Holborn Hill. – Has he not a rogue's face? Speak brother, 275
you understand physiognomy; a hanging look to me; of all
my boys the most unlike me; a has a damned Tyburn face,
without the benefit o'the clergy.

FORESIGHT
Hum, truly I don't care to discourage a young man; he has
a violent death in his face, but I hope no danger of hanging. 280

VALENTINE
Sir, is this usage for your son? For that old weather-headed
fool, I know how to laugh at him; but you, sir –

SIR SAMPSON
You, sir; and you, sir! Why, who are you, sir?

VALENTINE
Your son, sir.

SIR SAMPSON
That's more than I know, sir, and I believe not.   285

VALENTINE
Faith, I hope not.

SIR SAMPSON
What, would you have your mother a whore! Did you ever
hear the like! Did you ever hear the like! Body o'me –

VALENTINE
I would have an excuse for your barbarity and unnatural
usage.   290

SIR SAMPSON
Excuse! Impudence! Why, sirrah, mayn't I do what I
please? Are not you my slave? Did not I beget you? And
might not I have chosen whether I would have begot you or
no? Ouns, who are you? Whence came you? What brought
you into the world? How came you here, sir? Here, to stand 295
here, upon those two legs, and look erect with that auda-
cious face, hah? Answer me that? Did you come a volunteer
into the world? Or did I beat up for you with the lawful
authority of a parent, and press you to the service?

VALENTINE
I know no more why I came, than you do why you called 300
me. But here I am, and if you don't mean to provide for me,
I desire you would leave me as you found me.

---

275 *Holborn Hill* on the way to Tyburn gallows
277 *a has* (he has Q2–4, Ww)
278 *benefit o'the clergy* exemption from the law was granted for some offences to
      those who could read
298 *beat up for you … and* (om. Ww)

SIR SAMPSON

With all my heart: come, uncase, strip, and go naked out of
the world as you came into't.

VALENTINE

My clothes are soon put off; but you must also deprive me   305
of reason, thought, passions, inclinations, affections,
appetites, senses, and the huge train of attendants that you
begot along with me.

SIR SAMPSON

Body o'me, what a many-headed monster have I propa-
gated!   310

VALENTINE

I am of myself, a plain easy simple creature, and to be kept
at small expense; but the retinue that you gave me are crav-
ing and invincible; they are so many devils that you have
raised, and will have employment.

SIR SAMPSON

Ouns, what had I to do to get children? Can't a private man   315
be born without all these followers? Why, nothing under an
emperor should be born with appetites. Why, at this rate a
fellow that has but a groat in his pocket may have a stomach capable of a ten-shilling ordinary.

JEREMY

Nay, that's as clear as the sun; I'll make oath of it before   320
any justice in Middlesex.

SIR SAMPSON

Here's a cormorant too. – 'S'heart, this fellow was not born
with you? I did not beget him, did I?

JEREMY

By the provision that's made for me, you might have begot
me too: nay, and to tell your worship another truth, I   325
believe you did, for I find I was born with those same
whoreson appetites too, that my master speaks of.

SIR SAMPSON

Why, look you there now. I'll maintain it, that by the rule
of right reason, this fellow ought to have been born without a palate. 'S'heart, what should he do with a distin-   330
guishing taste? I warrant now he'd rather eat a pheasant
than a piece of poor John; and smell, now, why I warrant

303–4 *go naked … into't* 'Naked came I out of my mother's womb, and naked shall
     I return thither: the Lord gave, and the Lord hath taken away.' (Job I.21). This
     is part of The Order for the Burial of the Dead for the Church of England.
305 *deprive* (divest Ww)
319 *ordinary* eating house
322 *cormorant* glutton (the voracious seabird)
332 *poor John* dried or salted fish

he can smell, and loves perfumes above a stink. Why, there's it, and music – don't you love music, scoundrel?

JEREMY
Yes, I have a reasonable good ear, sir, as to jigs and country   335
dances, and the like; I don't much matter your solos or sonatas; they give me the spleen.

SIR SAMPSON
The spleen, ha, ha, ha! – a pox confound you, solos and sonatas? Ouns, whose son are you? How were you engendered, muckworm?   340

JEREMY
I am, by my father, the son of a chairman; my mother sold oysters in winter and cucumbers in summer; and I came upstairs into the world, for I was born in a cellar.

FORESIGHT
By your looks, you should go upstairs out of the world too, friend.   345

SIR SAMPSON
And if this rogue were anatomised now, and dissected, he has his vessels of digestion and concoction, and so forth, large enough for the inside of a cardinal, this son of a cucumber. These things are unaccountable and unreasonable. Body o'me, why was not I a bear, that my cubs might   350
have lived upon sucking their paws? Nature has been provident only to bears and spiders; the one has its nutriment in his own hands, and t'other spins his habitation out of his entrails.

VALENTINE
Fortune was provident enough to supply all the necessities   355
of my nature, if I had my right of inheritance.

SIR SAMPSON
Again! Ouns, han't you four thousand pound? If I had it again, I would not give thee a groat. What, wouldst thou have me turn pelican and feed thee out of my own vitals? 'S'heart, live by your wits. You were always fond of the   360
wits, now let's see if you have wit enough to keep yourself. Your brother will be in town tonight, or tomorrow morning, and then look you perform covenants, and so your friend and servant. – Come, brother Foresight.

                              Exeunt SIR SAMPSON *and* FORESIGHT

---

344 *go upstairs out of the world* be hanged
353–4 *his entrails* (his own entrails Ww)
359 *turn pelican* The legend of the pelican piercing its breast to feed its young with its blood was a traditional symbol of Christ's self-sacrifice.

JEREMY

I told you what your visit would come to.   365

VALENTINE

'Tis as much as I expected. I did not come to see him: I
came to Angelica; but since she was gone abroad, it was
easily turned another way, and at least looked well on my
side. – What's here? Mrs. Foresight and Mrs. Frail; they are
earnest. I'll avoid 'em. Come this way, and go and inquire   370
when Angelica will return.

[Exeunt]

Enter MRS. FORESIGHT *and* MRS. FRAIL

MRS. FRAIL

What have you to do to watch me? S'life, I'll do what I
please.

MRS. FORESIGHT

You will?

MRS. FRAIL

Yes, marry will I. A great piece of business to go to Covent   375
Garden Square in a hackney-coach and take a turn with
one's friend.

MRS. FORESIGHT

Nay, two or three turns, I'll take my oath.

MRS. FRAIL

Well, what if I took twenty? I warrant if you had been
there, it had been only innocent recreation. Lord, where's   380
the comfort of this life, if we can't have the happiness of
conversing where we like?

MRS. FORESIGHT

But can't you converse at home? I own it, I think there's no
happiness like conversing with an agreeable man; I don't
quarrel at that, nor I don't think but your conversation was   385
very innocent; but the place is public, and to be seen with a
man in a hackney-coach is scandalous: what if anybody else
should have seen you alight as I did? How can anybody be
happy, while they're in perpetual fear of being seen and
censured? Besides, it would not only reflect upon you,   390
sister, but me.

MRS. FRAIL

Pooh, here's a clutter. Why should it reflect upon you? I
don't doubt but you have thought yourself happy in a
hackney-coach before now. If I had gone to Knightsbridge,

394–5 *Knightsbridge … Barn-Elms* Knightsbridge and Chelsea village lay outside
London to the west. The 'new' Spring Garden (to distinguish it from the 'old'

or to Chelsea, or to Spring-Garden, or Barn-Elms with a   395
man alone, something might have been said.

MRS. FORESIGHT

Why, was I ever in any of these places? What do you mean,
sister?

MRS. FRAIL

Was I? What do you mean?

MRS. FORESIGHT

You have been at a worse place.   400

MRS. FRAIL

I at a worse place, and with a man!

MRS. FORESIGHT

I suppose you would not go alone to the *World's-End*?

MRS. FRAIL

The world's end! What, do you mean to banter me?

MRS. FORESIGHT

Poor innocent! You don't know that there's a place called
the *World's-End*? I'll swear you can keep your countenance   405
purely; you'd make an admirable player.

MRS. FRAIL

I'll swear you have a great deal of impudence, and in my
mind too much for the stage.

MRS. FORESIGHT

Very well, that will appear who has most. You never were
at the *World's-End*?   410

MRS. FRAIL

No.

MRS. FORESIGHT

You deny it positively to my face?

MRS. FRAIL

Your face, what's your face?

Spring Garden at Charing Cross) was over the river at Vauxhall. 'The ladies that
have an inclination to be private take delight in the close walks of Spring
Gardens, where both sexes meet and mutually serve one another as guides to lose
their way', Tom Brown, *Amusements Serious and Comical*, ed. cit. p. 40. Barn
Elms was a recreation ground up river at Mortlake (see Pepys, 26 May 1667).

397 *these* (those Ww)

402 *World's-End* At the corner of King's Road and World's End passage, Chelsea.
See William Gaunt, *Kensington and Chelsea*, London, B. T. Batsford (1975
edn.), pp. 55, 57 and 120. The author notes that there is an illustration in the
Gulston collection, Chelsea public library. It had a reputation as a place of
sexual assignation: 'Why, here's a Woman ... if she had a Vizard-Mask to
encourage me – I would go to the World's End with her', Thomas Southerne,
The Wives' Excuse I.ii.

407 *impudence* (confidence Ww)

MRS. FORESIGHT
No matter for that; it's as good a face as yours.

MRS. FRAIL
Not by a dozen years' wearing. – But I do deny it positively   415
to your face then.

MRS. FORESIGHT
I'll allow you now to find fault with my face; for I'll swear
your impudence has put me out of countenance: but look
you here now – where did you lose this gold bodkin? – O,
sister, sister!   420

MRS. FRAIL
My bodkin!

MRS. FORESIGHT
Nay, 'tis yours, look at it.

MRS. FRAIL
Well, if you go to that, where did you find this bodkin? O,
sister, sister! Sister every way.

MRS. FORESIGHT (*Aside*)
O devil on't, that I could not discover her without betray-   425
ing myself.

MRS. FRAIL
I have heard gentlemen say, sister, that one should take
great care when one makes a thrust in fencing, not to lie
open one's self.

MRS. FORESIGHT
It's very true, sister: well, since all's out, and as you say,   430
since we are both wounded, let us do that is often done in
duels, take care of one another, and grow better friends
than before.

MRS. FRAIL
With all my heart. Ours are but slight flesh wounds, and if
we keep 'em from air, not at all dangerous: well, give me   435
your hand in token of sisterly secrecy and affection.

MRS. FORESIGHT
Here 'tis with all my heart.

MRS. FRAIL
Well, as an earnest of friendship and confidence, I'll
acquaint you with a design that I have: to tell truth and
speak openly one to another, I'm afraid the world have   440
observed us more than we have observed one another. You
have a rich husband and are provided for; I am at a loss and
have no great stock either of fortune or reputation, and
therefore must look sharply about me. Sir Sampson has a

419 *bodkin* ornamental pin
431 *that* (what Ww)

son that is expected tonight, and by the account I have   445
heard of his education, can be no conjurer; the estate, you
know, is to be made over to him: now if I could wheedle
him, sister, ha? You understand me?

MRS. FORESIGHT

I do; and will help you to the utmost of my power. And I
can tell you one thing that falls out luckily enough: my   450
awkward daughter-in-law, who you know is designed for
his wife, is grown fond of Mr. Tattle; now if we can
improve that, and make her have an aversion for the booby,
it may go a great way towards his liking of you. Here they
come together; and let us contrive some way or other to   455
leave 'em together.

Enter TATTLE *and* MISS PRUE

MISS PRUE

Mother, mother, mother, look you here.

MRS. FORESIGHT

Fie, fie, miss, how you bawl. Besides, I have told you, you
must not call me mother.

MISS PRUE

What must I call you then? Are not you my father's wife?   460

MRS. FORESIGHT

Madam; you must say, madam. By my soul, I shall fancy
myself old indeed, to have this great girl call me mother.
Well, but, miss, what are you so overjoyed at?

MISS PRUE

Look you here, madam, then, what Mr. Tattle has given
me. Look you here, cousin, here's a snuff-box; nay, there's   465
snuff in't; – here, will you have any? – O good! How sweet
it is. – Mr. Tattle is all over sweet, his peruke is sweet, and
his gloves are sweet, and his handkerchief is sweet, pure
sweet, sweeter than roses. – Smell him, mother, madam, I
mean. He gave me this ring for a kiss.   470

TATTLE

O fie, miss, you must not kiss and tell.

MISS PRUE

Yes; I may tell my mother. – And he says he'll give me
something to make me smell so. – O, pray lend me your

---

451 *daughter-in-law* step-daughter
       for (to be Ww)
454 *liking of you* (liking you Ww)
460 *Are not you* (are you not Q3, 4, Ww)
467 *peruke* an artificial cap of hair

handkerchief. Smell, cousin. – He says he'll give me some- 475
thing that will make my smocks smell this way. Is not it
pure? It's better than lavender, mun. I'm resolved I won't
let nurse put any more lavender among my smocks, ha,
cousin?

MRS. FRAIL
Fie, miss; amongst your linen, you must say. You must
never say smock.   480

MISS PRUE
Why, it is not bawdy, is it, cousin?

TATTLE
O, madam, you are too severe upon miss; you must not find
fault with her pretty simplicity, it becomes her strangely. –
Pretty miss, don't let 'em persuade you out of your innocency.   485

MRS. FORESIGHT
O, damn you, toad! I wish you don't persuade her out of
her innocency.

TATTLE
Who, I, madam? O Lord, how can your ladyship have such
a thought? Sure, you don't know me?

MRS. FRAIL
Ah devil, sly devil. – He's as close, sister, as a confessor. He 490
thinks we don't observe him.

MRS. FORESIGHT
A cunning cur; how soon he could find out a fresh harmless
creature; and left us, sister, presently.

TATTLE
Upon reputation –

MRS. FORESIGHT
They're all so, sister, these men. They love to have the spoil- 495
ing of a young thing; they are as fond of it, as of being first
in the fashion, or of seeing a new play the first day. I warrant it would break Mr. Tattle's heart to think that anybody else should be beforehand with him.

TATTLE
O Lord, I swear I would not for the world –   500

MRS. FRAIL
O hang you; who'll believe you? You'd be hanged before
you'd confess. We know you. – She's very pretty! Lord,
what pure red and white! She looks so wholesome; ne'er
stir, I don't know, but I fancy, if I were a man –

MISS PRUE
How you love to jeer one, cousin.   505

MRS. FORESIGHT
Harkee, sister, by my soul, the girl is spoiled already. D'ye
think she'll ever endure a great lubberly tarpaulin? Gad, I

warrant you, she won't let him come near her after Mr.
Tattle.

MRS. FRAIL

O'my soul, I'm afraid not. Eh! filthy creature, that smells all   510
of pitch and tar! – Devil take you, you confounded toad,
why did you see her before she was married?

MRS. FORESIGHT

Nay, why did we let him? My husband will hang us. He'll
think we brought 'em acquainted.

MRS. FRAIL

Come, faith, let us be gone. If my brother Foresight should   515
find us with them, he'd think so, sure enough.

MRS. FORESIGHT

So he would. But then, leaving 'em together is as bad. And
he's such a sly devil, he'll never miss an opportunity.

MRS. FRAIL

I don't care; I won't be seen in't.

MRS. FORESIGHT

Well, if you should, Mr. Tattle, you'll have a world to   520
answer for. Remember I wash my hands of it; I'm thor-
oughly innocent.

Exeunt MRS. FORESIGHT *and* MRS. FRAIL

MISS PRUE

What makes 'em go away, Mr. Tattle? What do they mean?
Do you know?

TATTLE

Yes, my dear, I think I can guess. But hang me if I know the   525
reason of it.

MISS PRUE

Come, must not we go too?

TATTLE

No, no, they don't mean that.

MISS PRUE

No! What then? What shall you and I do together?

TATTLE

I must make love to you, pretty miss; will you let me make   530
love to you?

MISS PRUE

Yes, if you please.

TATTLE (*Aside*)

Frank, egad, at least. What a pox does Mrs. Foresight mean
by this civility? Is it to make a fool of me? Or does she leave

533 *pox* venereal disease

us together out of good morality, and do as she would be   535
done by? Gad, I'll understand it so.

MISS PRUE

Well, and how will you make love to me? Come, I long to
have you begin. Must I make love too? You must tell me
how.

TATTLE

You must let me speak miss, you must not speak first; I   540
must ask you questions, and you must answer.

MISS PRUE

What, is it like the catechism? Come then, ask me.

TATTLE

D'ye think you can love me?

MISS PRUE

Yes.

TATTLE

Pooh, pox, you must not say yes already; I shan't care a far-   545
thing for you then in a twinkling.

MISS PRUE

What must I say then?

TATTLE

Why, you must say no, or you believe not, or you can't tell.

MISS PRUE

Why, must I tell a lie then?

TATTLE

Yes, if you would be well-bred. All well-bred persons lie.   550
Besides, you are a woman; you must never speak what you
think; your words must contradict your thoughts; but your
actions may contradict your words. So, when I ask you if
you can love me, you must say no, but you must love me
too. If I tell you you are handsome, you must deny it, and   555
say I flatter you. But you must think yourself more charm-
ing than I speak you, and like me for the beauty which I say
you have as much as if I had it myself. If I ask you to kiss
me, you must be angry, but you must not refuse me. If I ask
you for more, you must be more angry, but more comply-   560
ing; and as soon as ever I make you say you'll cry out, you
must be sure to hold your tongue.

MISS PRUE

O Lord, I swear this is pure. I like it better than our old-
fashioned country way of speaking one's mind; and must
not you lie too?   565

550 *you would* (you'd Ww)
563 *pure* excellent

TATTLE
Hum – yes – but you must believe I speak truth.

MISS PRUE
O Gemini! Well, I always had a great mind to tell lies, but
they frighted me, and said it was a sin.

TATTLE
Well, my pretty creature; will you make me happy by giving
me a kiss?   570

MISS PRUE
No, indeed; I'm angry at you.   *Runs and kisses him*

TATTLE
Hold, hold, that's pretty well, but you should not have
given it me, but have suffered me to take it.

MISS PRUE
Well, we'll do it again.

TATTLE
With all my heart. Now then, my little angel.   *Kisses her* 575

MISS PRUE
Pish.

TATTLE
That's right. Again, my charmer.   *Kisses again*

MISS PRUE
O fie, nay, now I can't abide you.

TATTLE
Admirable! That was as well as if you had been born and
bred in Covent Garden all the days of your life; and won't 580
you show me, pretty miss, where your bedchamber is?

MISS PRUE
No, indeed won't I: but I'll run there, and hide myself from
you behind the curtains.

TATTLE
I'll follow you.

MISS PRUE
Ah, but I'll hold the door with both hands, and be angry;   585
and you shall push me down before you come in.

TATTLE
No, I'll come in first, and push you down afterwards.

MISS PRUE
Will you? Then I'll be more angry, and more complying.

TATTLE
Then I'll make you cry out.

MISS PRUE
O, but you shan't, for I'll hold my tongue.   590

573 *to take* (to have taken Ww)
580 *all ... life* (om. Ww)

TATTLE

O my dear, apt scholar.

MISS PRUE

Well, now I'll run and make more haste than you.   *Exit*

TATTLE

You shall not fly so fast, as I'll pursue.   *Exit after her*

Act III

Enter NURSE

NURSE

Miss, miss, Miss Prue. Mercy on me, marry and amen: why,
what's become of the child? Why miss, Miss Foresight! Sure
she has not locked herself up in her chamber and gone to
sleep, or to prayers. Miss, miss! I hear her. Come to your
father, child; open the door. Open the door, miss. I hear   5
you cry husht. O Lord, who's there? (*Peeps*) What's here to
do? O the Father! A man with her! Why, miss I say, God's
my life, here's fine doings towards – O Lord, we're all
undone. O you young harlotry. (*Knocks*) Od's my life,
won't you open the door? I'll come in the back way.   *Exit*   10

TATTLE *and* MISS PRUE *at the door*

MISS PRUE

O Lord, she's coming, and she'll tell my father. What shall
I do now?

TATTLE

Pox take her; if she had stayed two minutes longer, I should
have wished for her coming.

MISS PRUE

O dear, what shall I say? Tell me, Mr. Tattle, tell me a lie.   15

TATTLE

There's no occasion for a lie; I could never tell a lie to no
purpose. But since we have done nothing, we must say
nothing, I think. I hear her. I'll leave you together, and
come off as you can.

Thrusts her in, and shuts the door

Enter VALENTINE, SCANDAL, *and* ANGELICA

ANGELICA

You can't accuse me of inconstancy; I never told you that I   20
loved you.

VALENTINE

But I can accuse you of uncertainty, for not telling me
whether you did or no.

---

3 *has not* (has Ww)
10 s.d. *at the door* (om. Ww)
23 *or no* (or not Ww)

ANGELICA
  You mistake indifference for uncertainty; I never had con-
  cern enough to ask myself the question.   25
SCANDAL
  Nor good nature enough to answer him that did ask you;
  I'll say that for you, madam.
ANGELICA
  What, are you setting up for good nature?
SCANDAL
  Only for the affectation of it, as the women do for ill
  nature.   30
ANGELICA
  Persuade your friend that it is all affectation.
VALENTINE
  I shall receive no benefit from the opinion: for I know no
  effectual difference between continued affectation and
  reality.
TATTLE (*Coming up. Aside to* SCANDAL)
  Scandal, are you in private discourse, anything of secrecy?   35
SCANDAL
  Yes, but I dare trust you; we were talking of Angelica's love
  for Valentine. You won't speak of it?
TATTLE
  No, no, not a syllable. I know that's a secret, for it's whis-
  pered everywhere.
SCANDAL
  Ha, ha, ha.   40
ANGELICA
  What is, Mr. Tattle? I heard you say something was whis-
  pered everywhere.
SCANDAL
  Your love of Valentine.
ANGELICA
  How!
TATTLE
  No, madam, his love for your ladyship. Gad take me, I beg   45
  your pardon, for I never heard a word of your ladyship's
  passion till this instant.
ANGELICA
  My passion! And who told you of my passion, pray, sir?
SCANDAL
  Why, is the devil in you? Did not I tell it you for a secret?

32 s.p. VALENTINE (ANGELICA W1, SCANDAL W2)
37 *for Valentine* (to Valentine Ww)

TATTLE

  Gadso; but I thought she might have been trusted with her   50
own affairs.

SCANDAL

  Is that your discretion? Trust a woman with herself?

TATTLE

  You say true, I beg your pardon; I'll bring all off. – It was
impossible, madam, for me to imagine that a person of your
ladyship's wit and gallantry could have so long received the   55
passionate addresses of the accomplished Valentine, and
yet remain insensible; therefore, you will pardon me if from
a just weight of his merit, with your ladyship's good judgment, I formed the balance of a reciprocal affection.

VALENTINE

  O the devil, what damned costive poet has given thee this   60
lesson of fustian to get by rote?

ANGELICA

  I dare swear you wrong him; it is his own. And Mr. Tattle
only judges of the success of others from the effects of his
own merit. For certainly Mr. Tattle was never denied anything in his life.   65

TATTLE

  O Lord! yes indeed, madam, several times.

ANGELICA

  I swear I don't think 'tis possible.

TATTLE

  Yes, I vow and swear I have: Lord, madam, I'm the most
unfortunate man in the world, and the most cruelly used by
the ladies.   70

ANGELICA

  Nay, now you're ungrateful.

TATTLE

  No, I hope not. 'Tis as much ingratitude to own some
favours, as to conceal others.

VALENTINE

  There, now it's out.

ANGELICA

  I don't understand you now. I thought you had never asked   75
anything, but what a lady might modestly grant, and you
confess.

SCANDAL

  So, faith, your business is done here; now you may go brag
somewhere else.

---

60 *costive* constipated; slow in his mental processes
61 *fustian* pompous and empty talk

TATTLE
  Brag! O heavens! Why, did I name anybody?   80
ANGELICA
  No; I suppose that is not in your power; but you would if
  you could, no doubt on't.
TATTLE
  Not in my power, madam! What, does your ladyship mean,
  that I have no woman's reputation in my power?
SCANDAL (*Aside*)
  Ouns, why you won't own it, will you?   85
TATTLE
  Faith, madam, you're in the right; no more I have, as I hope
  to be saved; I never had it in my power to say anything to
  a lady's prejudice in my life. For as I was telling you,
  madam, I have been the most unsuccessful creature living in
  things of that nature, and never had the good fortune to be   90
  trusted once with a lady's secret, not once.
ANGELICA
  No?
VALENTINE
  Not once, I dare answer for him.
SCANDAL
  And I'll answer for him; for I'm sure if he had, he would
  have told me. I find, madam, you don't know Mr. Tattle.   95
TATTLE
  No indeed, madam, you don't know me at all I find: for
  sure my intimate friends would have known –
ANGELICA
  Then it seems you would have told, if you had been trusted.
TATTLE
  O pox, Scandal, that was too far put. – Never have told
  particulars, madam. Perhaps I might have talked as of a   100
  third person, or have introduced an amour of my own in
  conversation by way of novel; but never have explained
  particulars.
ANGELICA
  But whence comes the reputation of Mr. Tattle's secrecy, if
  he was never trusted?   105
SCANDAL
  Why thence it arises – the thing is proverbially spoken, but
  may be applied to him – as if we should say in general
  terms, he only is secret who never was trusted: a satirical
  proverb upon our sex. There's another upon yours: as she
  is chaste who was never asked the question. That's all.   110

109–10 *she is chaste ... question* from Ovid, *Amores* I.viii.43

VALENTINE

A couple of very civil proverbs, truly: 'tis hard to tell
whether the lady or Mr. Tattle be the more obliged to you.
For you found her virtue upon the backwardness of the
men, and his secrecy, upon the mistrust of the women.

TATTLE

Gad, it's very true, madam; I think we are obliged to acquit   115
ourselves. And for my part – but your ladyship is to speak
first –

ANGELICA

Am I? Well, I freely confess I have resisted a great deal of
temptation.

TATTLE

And I, gad, I have given some temptation that has not been   120
resisted.

VALENTINE

Good.

ANGELICA

I cite Valentine here, to declare to the court how fruitless he
has found his endeavours, and to confess all his solicitations and my denials.   125

VALENTINE

I am ready to plead, not guilty for you; and guilty for
myself.

SCANDAL

So, why this is fair, here's demonstration with a witness.

TATTLE

Well, my witnesses are not present. But I confess I have had
favours from persons – but as the favours are numberless,   130
so the persons are nameless.

SCANDAL

Pooh, pox, this proves nothing.

TATTLE

No? I can show letters, lockets, pictures, and rings, and if
there be occasion for witnesses, I can summon the maids at
the chocolate-houses, all the porters of Pall Mall and   135
Covent Garden, the doorkeepers at the playhouse, the
drawers at Locket's, Pontack's, the Rummer, Spring-

---

132 *pox* (om. Ww)
135 *porters of* (porters at Ww)
137 *drawers* tapsters; barmen
  Locket's ... Rummer eating houses. See Lord Foppington in Vanbrugh's *The
  Relapse* II.i. who goes 'to dinner at Locket's and there you are so nicely and delicately served, that ... they can compose you a dish, no bigger than a saucer,
  shall come to fifty shillings'.

Garden; my own landlady and *valet de chambre*; all who
shall make oath that I receive more letters than the secretary's office; and that I have more vizor-masks to inquire　140
for me than ever went to see the hermaphrodite or the
naked prince. And it is notorious that in a country church,
once, an inquiry being made who I was, it was answered, I
was the famous Tattle, who had ruined so many women.

VALENTINE

It was there, I suppose, you got the nickname of the Great　145
Turk.

TATTLE

True; I was called Turk-Tattle all over the parish. The next
Sunday all the old women kept their daughters at home,
and the parson had not half his congregation. He would
have brought me into the spiritual court, but I was revenged　150
upon him, for he had a handsome daughter whom I
initiated into the science. But I repented it afterwards, for it
was talked of in town – and a lady of quality that shall be
nameless, in a raging fit of jealousy, came down in her
coach and six horses, and exposed herself upon my　155
account; gad, I was sorry for it with all my heart. – You
know whom I mean – you know where we raffled –

SCANDAL

Mum, Tattle.

VALENTINE

S'death, are not you ashamed?

ANGELICA

O barbarous! I never heard so insolent a piece of vanity.　160
Fie, Mr. Tattle, I'll swear I could not have believed it. Is this
your secrecy?

TATTLE

Gadso, the heat of my story carried me beyond my discretion, as the heat of the lady's passion hurried her beyond
her reputation. But I hope you don't know whom I mean,　165
for there were a great many ladies raffled. – Pox on't, now
could I bite off my tongue.

139–40 *secretary's office* Secretary of State's office

140 *vizor-masks* masks were worn by ladies in public to protect their make-up or to
pass incognito. They were also recognised as signifying that the wearer was a
prostitute.

141–2 *hermaphrodite ... naked prince* popular shows of the day. The hermaphrodite was still living in Moorfields in 1693 (Davis). The prince was the son of a
'king of Moangis' (Summers).

145–6 *Great Turk* i.e. he kept a harem fit for a Sultan

SCANDAL

No, don't; for then you'll tell us no more. (*Goes to the door*) Come, I'll recommend a song to you upon the hint of my two proverbs, and I see one in the next room that will sing it.   170

TATTLE

For heaven's sake, if you do guess, say nothing. Gad, I'm very unfortunate.

Re-enter SCANDAL, *with one to sing*

SCANDAL

Pray sing the first song in the last new play.

SONG

Set by Mr. John Eccles

A nymph and a swain to Apollo once prayed;   175
The swain had been jilted, the nymph been betrayed;
Their intent was to try if his oracle knew
E'er a nymph that was chaste, or a swain that was true.

Apollo was mute, and had like t'have been posed,
But sagely at length he this secret disclosed: 180
He alone won't betray in whom none will confide,
And the nymph may be chaste that has never been tried.

Enter SIR SAMPSON, MRS. FRAIL, MISS PRUE, *and*
SERVANT

SIR SAMPSON

Is Ben come? Odso, my son Ben come? Odd, I'm glad on't. Where is he? I long to see him. Now, Mrs. Frail, you shall see my son Ben. Body o'me, he's the hopes of my family. I   185 han't seen him these three years. I warrant he's grown. Call him in; bid him make haste. I'm ready to cry for joy.

Exit SERVANT

MRS. FRAIL

Now, miss, you shall see your husband.

---

168 *don't* Q3, 4, Ww (doubt on't Q1, 2)
173 s.d. *Re-enter* SCANDAL, *with one to sing* (om. Ww)
174 *Eccles* (d. 1735) a popular composer for stage plays and operas including
     Congreve's *The Way of the World*, *The Judgment of Paris* and *Semele*
179 *posed* puzzled

MISS PRUE (*Aside to* MRS. FRAIL)
Pish, he shall be none of my husband.

MRS. FRAIL
Hush. Well, he shan't, leave that to me. – I'll beckon Mr.   190
Tattle to us.

ANGELICA
Won't you stay and see your brother?

VALENTINE
We are the twin stars and cannot shine in one sphere: when
he rises I must set. Besides, if I should stay, I don't know
but my father in good nature may press one to the immedi-   195
ate signing the deed of conveyance of my estate, and I'll
defer it so long as I can. Well, you'll come to a resolution.

ANGELICA
I can't. Resolution must come to me, or I shall never have
one.

SCANDAL
Come Valentine, I'll go with you; I've something in my   200
head to communicate to you.

Exit VALENTINE *and* SCANDAL

SIR SAMPSON
What, is my son Valentine gone? What, is he sneaked off
and would not see his brother? There's an unnatural whelp!
There's an ill-natured dog! What, were you here too,
madam, and could not keep him! Could neither love, nor   205
duty, nor natural affection oblige him? Odsbud, madam,
have no more to say to him; he is not worth your consideration. The rogue has not a dram of generous love about
him: all interest, all interest; he's an undone scoundrel, and
courts your estate: body o'me, he does not care a doit for   210
your person.

ANGELICA
I'm pretty even with him, Sir Sampson, for if ever I could
have liked anything in him, it should have been his estate
too. But since that's gone, the bait's off, and the naked
hook appears.   215

SIR SAMPSON
Odsbud, well spoken, and you are a wiser woman than I
thought you were; for most young women nowadays are to
be tempted with a naked hook.

---

193 *twin stars* Castor and Pollux. They were allowed by Zeus to dwell in Heaven on
     alternate days.
195 *one* Q1, 2 (me Q3, 4, Ww)
210 *doit* a Dutch coin worth almost nothing

ANGELICA
  If I marry, Sir Sampson, I'm for a good estate with any
  man, and for any man with a good estate; therefore, if I   220
  were obliged to make a choice, I declare, I'd rather have
  you than your son.

SIR SAMPSON
  Faith and troth, you're a wise woman, and I'm glad to hear
  you say so; I was afraid you were in love with the repro-
  bate. Odd, I was sorry for you with all my heart. Hang him,   225
  mongrel! Cast him off; you shall see the rogue show himself and make love to some desponding Cadua of fourscore
  for sustenance. Odd, I love to see a young spendthrift
  forced to cling to an old woman for support, like ivy round
  a dead oak. Faith, I do; I love to see 'em hug and cotton   230
  together, like down upon a thistle.

                 Enter BEN LEGEND *and* SERVANT

BEN
  Where's father?

SERVANT
  There, sir, his back's toward you.

SIR SAMPSON
  My son Ben! Bless thee, my dear boy; body o'me, thou art
  heartily welcome.   235

BEN
  Thank you, father, and I'm glad to see you.

SIR SAMPSON
  Odsbud, and I'm glad to see thee. Kiss me, boy; kiss me;
  again and again, dear Ben.   *Kisses him*

BEN
  So, so, enough, father. – Mess, I'd rather kiss these gentle-
  women.   240

SIR SAMPSON
  And so thou shalt. – Mrs. Angelica, my son Ben.

BEN
  Forsooth an you please. (*Salutes her*) Nay, mistress, I'm not
  for dropping anchor here; about ship, i'faith. (*Kisses* MRS.
  FRAIL) Nay, and you too, my little cockboat – so. (*Kisses*
  MISS PRUE)

TATTLE
  Sir, you're welcome ashore.   245

227 *Cadua* an obscure word, a windfall?
233 *toward* (towards W2)
242 *an you* (if you Ww)

BEN
Thank you, thank you, friend.

SIR SAMPSON
Thou hast been many a weary league, Ben, since I saw thee.

BEN
Ey, ey, been! Been far enough, an that be all. – Well, father,
and how do all at home? How does brother Dick, and
brother Val?   250

SIR SAMPSON
Dick, body o'me, Dick has been dead these two years; I writ
you word when you were at Leghorn.

BEN
Mess, and that's true; marry, I had forgot. Dick's dead, as
you say – well, and how? I have a many questions to ask
you. Well, you ben't married again, father, be you?   255

SIR SAMPSON
No, I intend you shall marry, Ben; I would not marry for
thy sake.

BEN
Nay, what does that signify? An you marry again – why
then, I'll go to sea again, so there's one for t'other, an that
be all. Pray don't let me be your hindrance; e'en marry, a   260
God's name, an the wind sit that way. As for my part,
mayhap I have no mind to marry.

MRS. FRAIL
That would be pity, such a handsome young gentleman.

BEN
Handsome! he, he, he, nay, forsooth, an you be for joking,
I'll joke with you, for I love my jest, an the ship were sink- 265
ing, as we sayn at sea. But I'll tell you why I don't much
stand towards matrimony. I love to roam about from port
to port, and from land to land: I could never abide to be
port-bound, as we call it. Now a man that is married has,
as it were, d'ye see, his feet in the bilboes, and mayhap   270
mayn't get 'em out again when he would.

SIR SAMPSON
Ben's a wag.

BEN
A man that is married, d'ye see, is no more like another
man, than a galley slave is like one of us free sailors; he is
chained to an oar all his life, and mayhap forced to tug a   275
leaky vessel into the bargain.

SIR SAMPSON
  A very wag, Ben's a very wag; only a little rough, he wants
  a little polishing.

MRS. FRAIL
  Not at all; I like his humour mightily, it's plain and honest.
  I should like such a humour in a husband extremely.   280

BEN
  Sayn you so, forsooth? Marry, and I should like such a
  handsome gentlewoman for a bedfellow hugely. How say
  you, mistress, would you like going to sea? Mess, you're a
  tight vessel and well rigged, and you were but as well
  manned.   285

MRS. FRAIL
  I should not doubt that, if you were master of me.

BEN
  But I'll tell you one thing, an you come to sea in a high
  wind, or that lady [*To* ANGELICA], you mayn't carry so
  much sail o'your head – top and top-gallant, by the mess.

MRS. FRAIL
  No, why so?   290

BEN
  Why an you do, you may run the risk to be overset, and
  then you'll carry your keels above water, he, he, he.

ANGELICA
  I swear, Mr. Benjamin is the veriest wag in nature; an
  absolute sea-wit.

SIR SAMPSON
  Nay, Ben has parts, but as I told you before, they want a   295
  little polishing: you must not take anything ill, madam.

BEN
  No, I hope the gentlewoman is not angry; I mean all in
  good part: for if I give a jest, I'll take a jest. And so forsooth
  you may be as free with me.

ANGELICA
  I thank you, sir, I am not at all offended; but methinks, Sir 300
  Sampson, you should leave him alone with his mistress. Mr.
  Tattle, we must not hinder lovers.

TATTLE (*Aside to* MISS PRUE)
  Well, miss, I have your promise.

SIR SAMPSON
  Body o'me, madam, you say true. Look you Ben; this is
  your mistress. Come miss, you must not be shamefaced;   305
  we'll leave you together.

---

289 *top and top-gallant* the sail set above the main mast and the sail above that

MISS PRUE

I can't abide to be left alone. Mayn't my cousin stay with me?

SIR SAMPSON

No, no. Come, let's away.

BEN

Look you father, mayhap the young woman mayn't take a   310
liking to me.

SIR SAMPSON

I warrant thee, boy. Come, come, we'll be gone; I'll venture
that.

Exeunt all but BEN *and* MISS PRUE

BEN

Come mistress, will you please to sit down, for an you
stand astern a that'n, we shall never grapple together.   315
Come, I'll haul a chair; there, an you please to sit, I'll sit by
you.

MISS PRUE

You need not sit so near one; if you have anything to say, I
can hear you farther off, I an't deaf.

BEN

Why, that's true, as you say, nor I an't dumb; I can be heard   320
as far as another. I'll heave off to please you. (*Sits farther
off*) An we were a league asunder, I'd undertake to hold
discourse with you, an 'twere not a main high wind indeed,
and full in my teeth. Look you forsooth, I am, as it were,
bound for the land of matrimony; 'tis a voyage, d'ye see,   325
that was none of my seeking. I was commanded by father,
and if you like of it, mayhap I may steer into your harbour.
How say you, mistress? The short of the thing is this, that
if you like me, and I like you, we may chance to swing in a
hammock together.   330

MISS PRUE

I don't know what to say to you, nor I don't care to speak
with you at all.

BEN

No, I'm sorry for that. But pray, why are you so scornful?

MISS PRUE

As long as one must not speak one's mind, one had better
not speak at all, I think, and truly I won't tell a lie for the   335
matter.

---

315 *astern a that'n* She has turned her back on him.
328 *is this, that* (is, that Ww)

BEN

Nay, you say true in that; it's but a folly to lie: for to speak
one thing and to think just the contrary way is, as it were,
to look one way, and to row another. Now, for my part,
d'ye see, I'm for carrying things above board, I'm not for   340
keeping anything under hatches; so that if you ben't as willing as I, say so, a God's name, there's no harm done;
mayhap you may be shamefaced; some maidens, tho'f they
love a man well enough, yet they don't care to tell'n so to's
face. If that's the case, why, silence gives consent.   345

MISS PRUE

But I'm sure it is not so, for I'll speak sooner than you
should believe that; and I'll speak truth, though one should
always tell a lie to a man; and I don't care, let my father do
what he will; I'm too big to be whipped, so I'll tell you
plainly, I don't like you, nor love you at all, nor never will,   350
that's more. So there's your answer for you, and don't
trouble me no more, you ugly thing.

BEN

Look you, young woman, you may learn to give good
words, however. I spoke you fair, d'ye see, and civil. As for
your love or your liking, I don't value it of a rope's end; and   355
mayhap I like you as little as you do me: what I said was in
obedience to father; gad, I fear a whipping no more than
you do. But I tell you one thing, if you should give such language at sea, you'd have a cat-o'-nine-tails laid cross your
shoulders. Flesh! who are you? You heard t'other hand-   360
some young woman speak civilly to me of her own accord.
Whatever you think of yourself, gad, I don't think you are
any more to compare to her, than a can of small beer to a
bowl of punch.

MISS PRUE

Well, and there's a handsome gentleman, and a fine gentle-   365
man, and a sweet gentleman, that was here that loves me,
and I love him; and if he sees you speak to me any more,
he'll thrash your jacket for you, he will, you great sea-calf.

BEN

What, do you mean that fair-weather spark that was here
just now? Will he thrash my jacket? Let'n – let'n. But an he   370
comes near me, mayhap I may giv'n a salt eel for's supper,
for all that. What does father mean to leave me alone as
soon as I come home with such a dirty dowdy? Sea-calf? I
an't calf enough to lick your chalked face, you cheese-curd

363 *small beer* weak beer
371 *salt eel* rope's end (a thrashing)

you. Marry thee! Ouns, I'll marry a Lapland witch as soon,   375
and live upon selling of contrary winds and wrecked
vessels.

MISS PRUE

I won't be called names, nor I won't be abused thus, so I
won't. If I were a man, (*Cries*) you durst not talk at this
rate. No, you durst not, you stinking tar-barrel.   380

Enter MRS. FORESIGHT *and* MRS. FRAIL

MRS. FORESIGHT

They have quarrelled just as we could wish.

BEN

Tar-barrel? Let your sweetheart there call me so, if he'll
take your part, your Tom Essence, and I'll say something to
him; gad, I'll lace his musk-doublet for him, I'll make him
stink; he shall smell more like a weasel than a civet cat afore   385
I ha' done with 'en.

MRS. FORESIGHT

Bless me, what's the matter? Miss – what, does she cry? –
Mr. Benjamin, what have you done to her?

BEN

Let her cry: the more she cries, the less she'll – She has been
gathering foul weather in her mouth, and now it rains out   390
at her eyes.

MRS. FORESIGHT

Come miss, come along with me, and tell me, poor child.

MRS. FRAIL

Lord, what shall we do? There's my brother Foresight and
Sir Sampson coming. Sister, do you take miss down into the
parlour, and I'll carry Mr. Benjamin into my chamber, for   395
they must not know that they are fallen out. Come sir, will
you venture yourself with me?   *Looks kindly on him*

BEN

Venture, mess, and that I will, though 'twere to sea in a
storm.

Exeunt

---

376 *selling of* (selling Ww)
383 *Tom Essence* 'a very Gaudy Crowd of *Odoriferous Tom-Essences* were Walking
    backwards and forwards with their Hats in their Hands, not daring to convert
    'em to their intended use, lest it should put the Foretops of their Wigs into some
    disorder', Ned Ward, *The London Spy* IX. See Thomas Rawlins's comedy *Tom
    Essence* (1677).
385 *civet cat* African and Asiatic animal from which the perfume civet was obtained
397 s.d. *Looks* (Looking Ww)

Enter SIR SAMPSON *and* FORESIGHT

SIR SAMPSON

I left 'em together here. What, are they gone? Ben's a brisk   400
boy: he has got her into a corner, father's own son! faith,
he'll tousle her, and mousle her: the rogue's sharp set,
coming from sea. If he should not stay for saying grace, old
Foresight, but fall to without the help of a parson, ha? Odd,
if he should, I could not be angry with him; 'twould be but   405
like me, a chip of the old block. Ha! thou'rt melancholy,
old prognostication; as melancholy as if thou hadst spilt the
salt or pared thy nails of a Sunday. Come cheer up, look
about thee. Look up, old stargazer. Now is he poring upon
the ground for a crooked pin, or an old horse-nail, with the   410
head towards him.

FORESIGHT

Sir Sampson, we'll have the wedding tomorrow morning.

SIR SAMPSON

With all my heart.

FORESIGHT

At ten o'clock, punctually at ten.

SIR SAMPSON

To a minute, to a second; thou shall set thy watch, and the   415
bridegroom shall observe its motions; they shall be married
to a minute, go to bed to a minute; and when the alarm
strikes, they shall keep time like the figures of St. Dunstan's
clock, and *consummatum est* shall ring all over the parish.

Enter SCANDAL

SCANDAL

Sir Sampson, sad news.   420

FORESIGHT

Bless us!

SIR SAMPSON

Why, what's the matter?

SCANDAL

Can't you guess at what ought to afflict you and him, and
all of us, more than anything else?

SIR SAMPSON

Body o'me, I don't know any universal grievance, but a   425

---

406 *melancholy* (melancholic Ww)
407 *melancholy* (melancholic Ww)
408 *of a* (on a Ww)
419 *consummatum est* Christ's dying words, 'It is finished'; here meaning the mar-
    riage is consummated

new tax and the loss of the Canary Fleet; without Popery
should be landed in the west, or the French fleet were at
anchor at Blackwall.

SCANDAL

No. Undoubtedly Mr. Foresight knew all this, and might
have prevented it.   430

FORESIGHT

'Tis no earthquake!

SCANDAL

No, not yet; nor whirlwind. But we don't know what it
may come to. But it has had a consequence already that
touches us all.

SIR SAMPSON

Why, body o'me, out with't.   435

SCANDAL

Something has appeared to your son Valentine. He's gone
to bed upon't, and very ill. He speaks little, yet says he has
a world to say; asks for his father and the wise Foresight;
talks of Raymond Lully, and the ghost of Lilly. He has
secrets to impart, I suppose, to you two. I can get nothing   440
out of him but sighs. He desires he may see you in the
morning, but would not be disturbed tonight, because he
has some business to do in a dream.

SIR SAMPSON

Hoity toity! What have I to do with his dreams or his divination? Body o'me, this is a trick to defer signing the con-   445
veyance. I warrant the devil will tell him in a dream that he
must not part with his estate: but I'll bring him a parson to
tell him that the devil's a liar. Or if that won't do, I'll bring
a lawyer that shall out-lie the devil. And so I'll try whether
my blackguard or his shall get the better of the day.   *Exit*   450

SCANDAL

Alas, Mr. Foresight, I'm afraid all is not right. You are a
wise man, and a conscientious man; a searcher into obscu-
rity and futurity; and if you commit an error, it is with a
great deal of consideration, and discretion, and caution.

---

426 *and* (or Ww) *without* (unless Ww)
       loss of the Canary Fleet England was at war with France.
428 *Blackwall* on the north bank of the Thames east of London and a major ship-
       yard
437 *yet says* (yet he says Ww)
439 *Lully* Raymond Lully (c. 1235–1316), Catalan mystic, poet and missionary to
       the Muslims
       Lilly William Lilly (1602–81), an English astrologer who published an annual
       almanac, which was continued 'after the manner of Mr. Lilly' after his death

FORESIGHT
Ah, good Mr. Scandal –   455

SCANDAL
Nay, nay, 'tis manifest; I do not flatter you. But Sir
Sampson is hasty, very hasty; I'm afraid he is not scrupu-
lous enough, Mr. Foresight. He has been wicked, and
heaven grant he may mean well in his affair with you – but
my mind misgives me, these things cannot be wholly insig-   460
nificant. You are wise, and should not be overreached,
methinks you should not –

FORESIGHT
Alas, Mr. Scandal, *humanum est errare.*

SCANDAL
You say true, man will err; mere man will err – but you are
something more. There have been wise men; but they were   465
such as you: men who consulted the stars and were
observers of omens. Solomon was wise, but how? – by his
judgment in astrology. So says Pineda in his third book and
eighth chapter.

FORESIGHT
You are learned, Mr. Scandal!   470

SCANDAL
A trifler, but a lover of art – and the wise men of the east
owed their instruction to a star, which is rightly observed
by Gregory the Great in favour of astrology! And Albertus
Magnus makes it the most valuable science, because, says
he, it teaches us to consider the causation of causes, in the   475
causes of things.

FORESIGHT
I protest I honour you, Mr. Scandal. I did not think you had
been read in these matters. Few young men are inclined –

SCANDAL
I thank my stars that have inclined me. But I fear this marriage and making over this estate, this transferring of a   480
rightful inheritance, will bring judgments upon us. I prophesy it, and I would not have the fate of Cassandra, not to
be believed. Valentine is disturbed; what can be the cause
of that? And Sir Sampson is hurried on by an unusual vio-
lence. I fear he does not act wholly from himself; methinks   485
he does not look as he used to.

---

468 *Pineda* Juan de (1558–1637), a Spanish Jesuit who wrote a commentary on
      Solomon, *De rebus Salomonis, libri VIII* (1609)
471 *of art* (of the art Q4)
473 *Gregory* Pope 590–604
473–4 *Albertus Magnus* (c. 1200–80) scholastic philosopher and polymath

FORESIGHT
He was always of an impetuous nature. But as to this marriage, I have consulted the science, and all appearances are
prosperous.

SCANDAL
Come, come, Mr. Foresight, let not the prospect of worldly   490
lucre carry you beyond your judgment, nor against your
conscience. You are not satisfied that you act justly.

FORESIGHT
How!

SCANDAL
You are not satisfied, I say. I am loath to discourage you,
but it is palpable that you are not satisfied.   495

FORESIGHT
How does it appear, Mr. Scandal? I think I am very well
satisfied.

SCANDAL
Either you suffer yourself to deceive yourself, or you do not
know yourself.

FORESIGHT
Pray explain yourself.   500

SCANDAL
Do you sleep well o'nights?

FORESIGHT
Very well.

SCANDAL
Are you certain? You do not look so.

FORESIGHT
I am in health, I think.

SCANDAL
So was Valentine this morning, and looked just so.   505

FORESIGHT
How! Am I altered any way! I don't perceive it.

SCANDAL
That may be, but your beard is longer than it was two
hours ago.

FORESIGHT
Indeed! Bless me.

Enter MRS. FORESIGHT

MRS. FORESIGHT
Husband, will you go to bed? It's ten o'clock. Mr. Scandal,   510
your servant.

488 *science* (stars Q3, 4, Ww)

SCANDAL

Pox on her, she has interrupted my design. But I must work
her into the project. – You keep early hours, madam.

MRS. FORESIGHT

Mr. Foresight is punctual; we sit up after him.

FORESIGHT

My dear, pray lend me your glass, your little looking glass.   515

SCANDAL

Pray lend it him, madam. I'll tell you the reason. (*She gives
him the glass;* SCANDAL *and she whisper*) My passion for
you is grown so violent – that I am no longer master of
myself. I was interrupted in the morning, when you had
charity enough to give me your attention, and I had hopes   520
of finding another opportunity of explaining myself to you,
but was disappointed all this day; and the uneasiness that
has attended me ever since brings me now hither at this
unseasonable hour.

MRS. FORESIGHT

Was there ever such impudence, to make love to me before   525
my husband's face? I'll swear I'll tell him.

SCANDAL

Do, I'll die a martyr, rather than disclaim my passion. But
come a little farther this way, and I'll tell you what project
I had to get him out of the way, that I might have an opportunity of waiting upon you.   *Whisper*   530

FORESIGHT (*Looking in the glass*)

I do not see any revolution here. Methinks I look with a
serene and benign aspect – pale, a little pale – but the roses
of these cheeks have been gathered many years. Ha! I do
not like that sudden flushing – gone already! Hem, hem,
hem! faintish. My heart is pretty good – yet it beats; and my   535
pulses, ha! – I have none – mercy on me! Hum – yes, here
they are. Gallop, gallop, gallop, gallop, gallop, gallop, hey!
Whither will they hurry me? Now they're gone again. And
now I'm faint again; and pale again, and hem! and my hem!
– breath, hem! – grows short; hem! hem! he, he, hem!   540

SCANDAL

It takes; pursue it in the name of love and pleasure.

MRS. FORESIGHT

How do you do, Mr. Foresight?

FORESIGHT

Hum, not so well as I thought I was. Lend me your hand.

SCANDAL

Look you there now. Your lady says your sleep has been
unquiet of late.   545

FORESIGHT

Very likely.

MRS. FORESIGHT

O, mighty restless, but I was afraid to tell him so. He has been subject to talking and starting.

SCANDAL

And did not use to be so.

MRS. FORESIGHT

Never, never; till within these three nights; I cannot say that   550
he has once broken my rest since we have been married.

FORESIGHT

I will go to bed.

SCANDAL

Do so, Mr. Foresight, and say your prayers. He looks better then he did.

MRS. FORESIGHT

Nurse, nurse!   *Calls*   555

FORESIGHT

Do you think so, Mr. Scandal?

SCANDAL

Yes, yes, I hope this will be gone by morning, taking it in time.

FORESIGHT

I hope so.

Enter NURSE

MRS. FORESIGHT

Nurse, your master is not well; put him to bed.   560

SCANDAL

I hope you will be able to see Valentine in the morning. You had best take a little diacodium and cowslip water, and lie upon your back; maybe you may dream.

FORESIGHT

I thank you, Mr. Scandal, I will. – Nurse, let me have a watch-light, and lay the *Crumbs of Comfort* by me.   565

NURSE

Yes, sir.

FORESIGHT

And – hem, hem! I am very faint.

SCANDAL

No, no, you look much better.

FORESIGHT

Do I? [*To* NURSE] And d'ye hear – bring me, let me see –

557 *taking* (take W2)
562 *diacodium* syrup of poppies
565 *Crumbs of Comfort* (?1626) by Michael Sparke (d. 1653). A popular manual of
       devotion which had reached a 'forty-third' edition by 1726.

within a quarter of twelve – hem – he – hem! – just upon   570
the turning of the tide, bring me the urinal; and I hope
neither the lord of my ascendant nor the moon will be combust; and then I may do well.

SCANDAL
I hope so. Leave that to me; I will erect a scheme; and I
hope I shall find both Sol and Venus in the sixth house.   575

FORESIGHT
I thank you, Mr. Scandal. Indeed, that would be a great
comfort to me. Hem, hem! Good night.   *Exit*

SCANDAL
Good night, good Mr. Foresight; and I hope Mars and
Venus will be in conjunction – while your wife and I are
together.   580

MRS. FORESIGHT
Well; and what use do you hope to make of this project?
You don't think that you are ever like to succeed in your
design upon me?

SCANDAL
Yes, faith I do; I have a better opinion both of you and
myself than to despair.   585

MRS. FORESIGHT
Did you ever hear such a toad? Harkee devil; do you think
any woman honest?

SCANDAL
Yes, several, very honest; they'll cheat a little at cards,
sometimes, but that's nothing.

MRS. FORESIGHT
Pshaw! but virtuous, I mean.   590

SCANDAL
Yes, faith, I believe some women are virtuous too; but 'tis
as I believe some men are valiant, through fear. For why
should a man court danger, or a woman shun pleasure?

---

572 *lord of my ascendant* 'Let the Lord of the ascendant and the Moon ... be free
     from Impediment' when giving physic, Ramesey, *Astrologie Restored*, III.ii.63
     (Davis)

572–3 *combust* close to the sun, thus having their influence destroyed

575 *sixth house* the 'houses' represent the parts of everyday life in which astrological
     forces work. According to William Lilly's *Merlinus Anglicus Junior* (1644) the
     sixth house relates to sickness, servants and little cattle. Foresight thinks the
     presence of Venus (Love) the 'ruler' of the 'house' and Sol (the Sun and a signi-
     fier of divine monarchy) will be favourable for his health. But Scandal's 'scheme'
     envisages another kind of 'erection'.

578–9 *Mars and Venus* alluding to the betrayal by Venus of her husband, Vulcan,
     with Mars

MRS. FORESIGHT
O monstrous! What are conscience and honour?

SCANDAL
Why, honour is a public enemy, and conscience a domestic   595
thief; and he that would secure his pleasure must pay a trib-
ute to one, and go halves with the t'other. As for honour,
that you have secured, for you have purchased a perpetual
opportunity for pleasure.

MRS. FORESIGHT
An opportunity for pleasure!   600

SCANDAL
Aye, your husband. A husband is an opportunity for pleasure, so you have taken care of honour, and 'tis the least I
can do to take care of conscience.

MRS. FORESIGHT
And so you think we are free for one another?

SCANDAL
Yes, faith, I think so; I love to speak my mind.   605

MRS. FORESIGHT
Why then, I'll speak my mind. Now, as to this affair
between you and me. Here you make love to me; why, I'll
confess it does not displease me. Your person is well
enough, and your understanding is not amiss.

SCANDAL
I have no great opinion of myself; yet I think I'm neither   610
deformed, nor a fool.

MRS. FORESIGHT
But you have a villainous character; you are a libertine in
speech as well as practice.

SCANDAL
Come, I know what you would say. You think it more dangerous to be seen in conversation with me, than to allow   615
some other men the last favour. You mistake; the liberty I
take in talking is purely affected for the service of your sex.
He that first cries out stop thief, is often he that has stolen
the treasure. I am a juggler that acts by confederacy; and if
you please, we'll put a trick upon the world.   620

MRS. FORESIGHT
Aye, but you are such a universal juggler – that I'm afraid
you have a great many confederates.

SCANDAL
Faith, I'm sound.

---

597 *with the t'other* (with t'other Q3, 4, Ww)
610 *yet I* (but I Ww)
623 *sound* free from venereal disease

MRS. FORESIGHT

O fie – I'll swear you're impudent.

SCANDAL

I'll swear you're handsome.   625

MRS. FORESIGHT

Pish, you'd tell me so, though you did not think so.

SCANDAL

And you'd think so, though I should not tell you so: and
now I think we know one another pretty well.

MRS. FORESIGHT

O Lord, who's here?

Enter MRS. FRAIL *and* BEN

BEN

Mess, I love to speak my mind. Father has nothing to do   630
with me. Nay, I can't say that neither; he has something to
do with me. But what does that signify? If so be that I ben't
minded to be steered by him, 'tis as tho'f he should strive
against wind and tide.

MRS. FRAIL

Aye, but, my dear, we must keep it secret, till the estate be   635
settled; for you know, marrying without an estate is like
sailing in a ship without ballast.

BEN

He, he, he; why, that's true; just so, for all the world it is
indeed, as like as two cable ropes.

MRS. FRAIL

And though I have a good portion, you know one would   640
not venture all in one bottom.

BEN

Why, that's true again; for mayhap one bottom may spring
a leak. You have hit it indeed; mess, you've nicked the
channel.

MRS. FRAIL

Well, but if you should forsake me after all, you'd break my   645
heart.

BEN

Break your heart? I'd rather the *Marigold* should break her
cable in a storm, as well as I love her. Flesh, you don't think
I'm false-hearted like a landman? A sailor will be honest,
tho'f mayhap he has never a penny of money in his pocket.   650
Mayhap I may not have so fair a face as a citizen or a
courtier; but for all that, I've as good blood in my veins,
and a heart as sound as a biscuit.

624 *you're* (your Q1 uncorr. cited by Davis)

MRS. FRAIL

And will you love me always?

BEN

Nay, an I love once, I'll stick like pitch; I'll tell you that. 655
Come, I'll sing you a song of a sailor.

MRS. FRAIL

Hold, there's my sister; I'll call her to hear it.

MRS. FORESIGHT (*To* SCANDAL)

Well, I won't go to bed to my husband tonight, because I'll
retire to my own chamber and think of what you have said.

SCANDAL

Well, you'll give me leave to wait upon you to your cham- 660
ber door, and leave you my last instructions.

MRS. FORESIGHT

Hold, here's my sister coming toward us.

MRS. FRAIL

If it won't interrupt you, I'll entertain you with a song.

BEN

The song was made upon one of our ship's crew's wife; our
boatswain made the song; mayhap you may know her, sir. 665
Before she was married, she was called buxom Joan of
Deptford.

SCANDAL

I have heard of her.

BEN *sings*

BALLAD
Set by Mr. John Eccles

A soldier and a sailor,
A tinker, and a tailor,   670
Had once a doubtful strife, sir,
To make a maid a wife, sir,
Whose name was buxom Joan.
For now the time was ended,
When she no more intended,   675
To lick her lips at men, sir,
And gnaw the sheets in vain, sir,
And lie o'nights alone.

The soldier swore like thunder,
He loved her more than plunder;   680
And showed her many a scar, sir,
That he had brought from far, sir,

662 *toward* (towards Ww)
666 *was married* (married W2)

With fighting for her sake.
The tailor thought to please her,
With off'ring her his measure. 685
The tinker too with mettle,
Said he could mend her kettle,
And stop up ev'ry leak.

But while these three were prating,
The sailor slyly waiting, 690
Thought if it came about, sir,
That they should all fall out, sir:
He then might play his part.
And just e'en as he meant, sir,
To loggerheads they went, sir, 695
And then he let fly at her,
A shot 'twixt wind and water,
That won this fair maid's heart.

If some of our crew that came to see me are not gone, you
shall see that we sailors can dance sometimes as well as 700
other folks. (*Whistles*) I warrant that brings 'em, an they be
within hearing.

Enter SEAMEN

O, here they be – and fiddles along with 'em. Come my
lads, let's have a round, and I'll make one.

Dance

We're merry folk, we sailors; we han't much to care for. 705
Thus we live at sea: eat biscuit, and drink flip, put on a
clean shirt once a quarter, come home and lie with our
landladies once a year, get rid of a little money; and then
put off with the next fair wind. How d'ye like us?

MRS. FRAIL
O, you are the happiest, merriest men alive. 710

MRS. FORESIGHT
We're beholding to Mr. Benjamin for this entertainment. I
believe it's late.

BEN
Why, forsooth, an you think so, you had best go to bed. For
my part, I mean to toss a can, and remember my sweetheart, afore I turn in; mayhap I may dream of her. 715

---

685 *measure* i) his yard ii) penis
706 *flip* a hot drink of sweetened beer and spirits
711 *beholding* (beholden Ww)

MRS. FORESIGHT
  Mr. Scandal, you had best go to bed and dream too.
SCANDAL
  Why, faith, I have a good lively imagination, and can dream
  as much to the purpose as another, if I set about it: but
  dreaming is the poor retreat of a lazy, hopeless, and imperfect lover; 'tis the last glimpse of love to worn-out sinners,   720
  and the faint dawning of a bliss to wishing girls and grow-
  ing boys.
     There's nought but willing, waking love, that can
     Make blest the ripened maid, and finished man.

                                                    Exeunt

Act IV

VALENTINE'S *lodging*

Enter SCANDAL *and* JEREMY

SCANDAL
Well, is your master ready? Does he look madly, and talk
madly?

JEREMY
Yes, sir; you need make no great doubt of that; he that was
so near turning poet yesterday morning can't be much to
seek in playing the madman today.   5

SCANDAL
Would he have Angelica acquainted with the reason of his
design?

JEREMY
No, sir, not yet. He has a mind to try whether his playing
the madman won't make her play the fool, and fall in love
with him; or at least own that she has loved him all this   10
while and concealed it.

SCANDAL
I saw her take coach just now with her maid, and think I
heard her bid the coachman drive hither.

JEREMY
Like enough, sir, for I told her maid this morning my
master was run stark mad only for love of her mistress. I   15
hear a coach stop; if it should be she, sir, I believe he would
not see her till he hears how she takes it.

SCANDAL
Well, I'll try her. – 'Tis she, here she comes.

Enter ANGELICA *with* JENNY

ANGELICA
Mr. Scandal, I suppose you don't think it a novelty to see a
woman visit a man at his own lodgings in a morning?   20

SCANDAL
Not upon a kind occasion, madam. But when a lady comes
tyrannically to insult a ruined lover, and make manifest the
cruel triumphs of her beauty, the barbarity of it something
surprises me.

ANGELICA
I don't like raillery from a serious face. Pray tell me what is 25
the matter?

JEREMY
No strange matter, madam; my master's mad, that's all. I
suppose your ladyship has thought him so a great while.

ANGELICA
How d'ye mean, mad?
JEREMY
Why, faith, madam, he's mad for want of his wits, just as   30
he was for want of money; his head is e'en as light as his
pockets, and anybody that has a mind to a bad bargain
can't do better than to beg him for his estate.
ANGELICA
If you speak truth, your endeavouring at wit is very unsea-
sonable –   35
SCANDAL (*Aside*)
She's concerned, and loves him.
ANGELICA
Mr. Scandal, you can't think me guilty of so much inhu-
manity as not to be concerned for a man I must own myself
obliged to – pray tell me truth.
SCANDAL
Faith, madam, I wish telling a lie would mend the matter.   40
But this is no new effect of an unsuccessful passion.
ANGELICA (*Aside*)
I know not what to think. Yet I should be vexed to have a
trick put upon me. – May I not see him?
SCANDAL
I'm afraid the physician is not willing you should see him
yet. – Jeremy, go in and inquire.   45

Exit JEREMY

ANGELICA (*Aside*)
Ha! I saw him wink and smile. I fancy 'tis a trick! I'll try. –
I would disguise to all the world a failing, which I must
own to you. I fear my happiness depends upon the recovery
of Valentine. Therefore I conjure you, as you are his friend,
and as you have compassion upon one fearful of affliction,   50
to tell me what I am to hope for. – I cannot speak. – But
you may tell me; tell me, for you know what I would ask.
SCANDAL (*Aside*)
So, this is pretty plain. – Be not too much concerned,
madam; I hope his condition is not desperate: an acknowledgment of love from you, perhaps, may work a cure, as   55
the fear of your aversion occasioned his distemper.
ANGELICA (*Aside*)
Say you so; nay, then I'm convinced: and if I don't play
trick for trick, may I never taste the pleasure of revenge. –

31 *was for* (was poor for Q3, 4, Ww)
39 *tell me truth* (tell me the truth W2)
52 *tell me; tell me, for* (tell me, for W2)

Acknowledgment of love! I find you have mistaken my
compassion, and think me guilty of a weakness I am a   60
stranger to. But I have too much sincerity to deceive you,
and too much charity to suffer him to be deluded with vain
hopes. Good nature and humanity oblige me to be concerned for him; but to love is neither in my power nor inclination; and if he can't be cured without I suck the poison   65
from his wounds, I'm afraid he won't recover his senses till
I lose mine.

SCANDAL
Hey, brave woman, i'faith – won't you see him then, if he
desire it?

ANGELICA
What signify a madman's desires? Besides, 'twould make   70
me uneasy. If I don't see him, perhaps my concern for him
may lessen. If I forget him, 'tis no more than he has done
by himself; and now the surprise is over, methinks I am not
half so sorry for him as I was.

SCANDAL
So, faith, good nature works apace; you were confessing   75
just now an obligation to his love.

ANGELICA
But I have considered that passions are unreasonable and
involuntary; if he loves, he can't help it; and if I don't love,
I can't help it; no more than he can help his being a man,
or I my being a woman; or no more than I can help my   80
want of inclination to stay longer here. – Come, Jenny.

Exit ANGELICA *and* JENNY

SCANDAL
Humph! An admirable composition, faith, this same
womankind.

Enter JEREMY

JEREMY
What, is she gone, sir?

SCANDAL
Gone! Why, she was never here, nor anywhere else; nor I   85
don't know her if I see her, nor you neither.

JEREMY
Good lack! What's the matter now? Are any more of us to
be mad? Why, sir, my master longs to see her, and is almost
mad in good earnest with the joyful news of her being here.

SCANDAL
We are all under a mistake. Ask no questions, for I can't   90

74 *sorry for him as* (sorry as Q3, 4, Ww)

resolve you; but I'll inform your master. In the meantime, if
our project succeed no better with his father than it does
with his mistress, he may descend from his exaltation of
madness into the road of common sense, and be content
only to be made a fool with other reasonable people. I hear   95
Sir Sampson. You know your cue; I'll to your master. *Exit*

Enter SIR SAMPSON LEGEND *with* [BUCKRAM] *a lawyer*

SIR SAMPSON

D'ye see, Mr. Buckram, here's the paper signed with his
own hand.

BUCKRAM

Good, sir. And the conveyance is ready drawn in this box,
if he be ready to sign and seal.   100

SIR SAMPSON

Ready, body o'me, he must be ready; his sham sickness
shan't excuse him. – O, here's his scoundrel. Sirrah, where's
your master?

JEREMY

Ah, sir, he's quite gone.

SIR SAMPSON

Gone! What, he is not dead?   105

JEREMY

No, sir, not dead.

SIR SAMPSON

What, is he gone out of town, run away, ha! Has he tricked
me? Speak, varlet.

JEREMY

No, no, sir; he's safe enough, sir, an he were but as sound,
poor gentleman. He is indeed here, sir, and not here, sir.   110

SIR SAMPSON

Hey day, rascal, do you banter me? Sirrah, d'ye banter me?
Speak, sirrah, where is he, for I will find him.

JEREMY

Would you could, sir, for he has lost himself. Indeed, sir, I
have almost broke my heart about him. – I can't refrain
tears when I think of him, sir; I'm as melancholy for him as   115
a passing-bell, sir, or a horse in a pound.

SIR SAMPSON

A pox confound your similitudes, sir. Speak to be understood, and tell me in plain terms what the matter is with
him, or I'll crack your fool's skull.

114 *almost* Ww (a most Q1–4)
116 *passing-bell* the bell which marked a funeral
     pound an enclosure for stray animals

JEREMY

Ah, you've hit it, sir; that's the matter with him, sir; his   120
skull's cracked, poor gentleman; he's stark mad, sir.

SIR SAMPSON

Mad!

BUCKRAM

What, is he *non compos*?

JEREMY

Quite *non compos*, sir.

BUCKRAM

Why, then all's obliterated, Sir Sampson. If he be *non*   125
compos mentis, his act and deed will be of no effect; it is
not good in law.

SIR SAMPSON

Ouns, I won't believe it; let me see him, sir. – Mad! I'll
make him find his senses.

JEREMY

Mr. Scandal is with him, sir; I'll knock at the door.   130

> *Goes to the scene, which opens and discovers*
> VALENTINE *upon a couch disorderly dressed*, SCANDAL
> *by him*

SIR SAMPSON

How now, what's here to do?

VALENTINE (*Starting*)

Ha! Who's that?

SCANDAL

For heaven's sake, softly, sir, and gently; don't provoke
him.

VALENTINE

Answer me; who is that? and that?   135

SIR SAMPSON

Gads bobs, does he not know me? Is he mischievous? I'll
speak gently. – Val, Val, dost thou not know me, boy? Not
know thy own father, Val! I am thy own father, and this is
honest Brief Buckram the lawyer.

VALENTINE

It may be so – I did not know you. – The world is full. –   140
There are people that we do know, and people that we do
not know; and yet the sun shines upon all alike. There are
fathers that have many children, and there are children that
have many fathers. – 'Tis strange! But I am Truth, and
come to give the world the lie.   145

---

123 *non compos* short for *non compos mentis*, not of sound mind
138–9 *this is honest* (this honest W2)

SIR SAMPSON
Body o'me, I know not what to say to him.

VALENTINE
Why does that lawyer wear black? Does he carry his conscience withoutside? – Lawyer, what are thou? Dost thou
know me?

BUCKRAM
O Lord, what must I say? – Yes, sir.   150

VALENTINE
Thou liest, for I am Truth. 'Tis hard I cannot get a liveli-
hood amongst you. I have been sworn out of Westminster
Hall the first day of every term. Let me see – no matter how
long. But I'll tell you one thing; it's a question that would
puzzle an arithmetician if you should ask him: whether the   155
Bible saves more souls in Westminster Abbey, or damns
more in Westminster Hall. For my part, I am Truth, and
can't tell; I have very few acquaintance.

SIR SAMPSON
Body o'me, he talks sensibly in his madness. – Has he no
intervals?   160

JEREMY
Very short, sir.

BUCKRAM
Sir, I can do you no service while he's in this condition;
here's your paper, sir. He may do me a mischief if I stay.
The conveyance is ready, sir, if he recover his senses. *Exit*

SIR SAMPSON
Hold, hold, don't you go yet.   165

SCANDAL
You'd better let him go, sir, and send for him if there be
occasion, for I fancy his presence provokes him more.

VALENTINE
Is the lawyer gone? 'Tis well. Then we may drink about
without going together by the ears. Heigh ho! What o'clock
is't? My father here! Your blessing, sir?   170

SIR SAMPSON
He recovers. – Bless thee, Val. How dost thou do, boy?

VALENTINE
Thank you, sir, pretty well. I have been a little out of order.
Won't you please to sit, sir?

SIR SAMPSON
Aye, boy. Come, thou shalt sit down by me.

152–3 *Westminster Hall* the principal law court
169 *going together by the ears* quarreling

VALENTINE
    Sir, 'tis my duty to wait.   175

SIR SAMPSON
    No, no, come, come, sit you down, honest Val. How dost
thou do? Let me feel thy pulse. O, pretty well now, Val.
Body o'me, I was sorry to see thee indisposed; but I'm glad
thou'rt better, honest Val.

VALENTINE
    I thank you, sir.   180

SCANDAL (*Aside*)
    Miracle! The monster grows loving.

SIR SAMPSON
    Let me feel thy hand again, Val. It does not shake. I believe
thou canst write, Val: ha, boy? Thou canst write thy name,
Val? (*In a whisper to* JEREMY) Jeremy, step and overtake
Mr. Buckram; bid him make haste back with the con-   185
veyance – quick – quick.

                                                Exit JEREMY

SCANDAL (*Aside*)
    That ever I should suspect such a heathen of any remorse!

SIR SAMPSON
    Dost thou know this paper, Val? I know thou'rt honest and
wilt perform articles.
        Shows him the paper, but holds it out of his reach

VALENTINE
    Pray let me see it, sir. You hold it so far off that I can't tell   190
whether I know it or no.

SIR SAMPSON
    See it, boy? Aye, aye, why thou dost see it. 'Tis thy own
hand, Val. Why, let me see, I can read it as plain as can be:
look you here, (*Reads*) *The condition of this obligation* –
Look you, as plain as can be, so it begins, and then at the   195
bottom, *As witness my hand*, VALENTINE LEGEND, in great
letters. Why, 'tis as plain as the nose in one's face; what, are
my eyes better than thine? I believe I can read it farther off
yet – let me see.   *Stretches his arm as far as he can*

VALENTINE
    Will you please to let me hold it, sir?   200

SIR SAMPSON
    Let thee hold it, sayst thou? Aye, with all my heart. What
matter is it who holds it? What need anybody hold it? I'll

---

176 *sit you* (sit thee Ww)
181 *monster* the name by which Caliban is often addressed in *The Tempest*
193 *Val* (Vally Ww)

put it up in my pocket, Val, and then nobody need hold it.
(*Puts the paper in his pocket*) There Val: it's safe enough,
boy. But thou shalt have it as soon as thou has set thy hand   205
to another paper, little Val.

Re-enter JEREMY *with* BUCKRAM

VALENTINE

What, is my bad genius here again! O no, 'tis the lawyer
with an itching palm, and he's come to be scratched. My
nails are not long enough. Let me have a pair of red-hot
tongs quickly, quickly, and you shall see me act St.   210
Dunstan, and lead the devil by the nose.

BUCKRAM

O Lord, let me be gone; I'll not venture myself with a
madman.   *Exit*

VALENTINE

Ha, ha, ha, you need not run so fast; honesty will not overtake you. Ha, ha, ha, the rogue found me out to be *in forma*   215
pauperis presently.

SIR SAMPSON

Ouns! What a vexation is here! I know not what to do, or
say, nor which way to go.

VALENTINE

Who's that, that's out of his way? – I am Truth, and can set
him right. Harkee, friend, the straight road is the worst way   220
you can go. He that follows his nose always will very often
be led into a stink. *Probatum est*. But what are you for?
Religion or politics? There's a couple of topics for you, no
more like one another than oil and vinegar; and yet those
two beaten together by a state-cook make sauce for the   225
whole nation.

SIR SAMPSON

What the devil had I to do ever to beget sons? Why did I
ever marry?

VALENTINE

Because thou wert a monster, old boy: the two greatest
monsters in the world are a man and a woman. What's thy   230
opinion?

SIR SAMPSON

Why, my opinion is, that those two monsters joined
together make yet a greater, that's a man and his wife.

---

207 *bad genius* Perhaps an allusion to the appearance of Caesar's ghost, *Julius
    Caesar*, IV.iii.281.
215–16 *in forma pauperis* legally not liable for costs because of poverty
222 *Probatum est* It is a tried and tested thing

VALENTINE
    Aha! Old truepenny, sayst thou so? Thou hast nicked it.
    But it's wonderful strange, Jeremy.   235
JEREMY
    What is, sir?
VALENTINE
    That grey hairs should cover a green head – and I make a
    fool of my father.

            Enter FORESIGHT, MRS. FORESIGHT *and* MRS. FRAIL

    What's here? *Erra pater*? Or a bearded sybil? If Prophecy
    comes, Truth must give place.   240

                                        Exit with JEREMY

FORESIGHT
    What says he? What, did he prophesy? Ha, Sir Sampson,
    bless us! How are we?
SIR SAMPSON
    Are we? A pox o' your prognostication. Why, we are fools
    as we use to be. Ouns, that you could not foresee that the
    moon would predominate, and my son be mad. Where's   245
    your oppositions, your trines, and your quadrates? What
    did your Cardan and your Ptolemy tell you? Your
    Messahalah and your Longomontanus, your harmony of
    chiromancy with astrology. Ah! pox on't, that I that know
    the world, and men and manners, that don't believe a syl-   250
    lable in the sky and stars, and sun and almanacs, and trash,
    should be directed by a dreamer, an omen-hunter, and defer
    business in expectation of a lucky hour, when, body o'me,
    there never was a lucky hour after the first opportunity.

                                                            Exit

234 *truepenny* the name by which Hamlet calls his father's ghost, *Hamlet* II.i.150.
      See also *Spectator* 82 where Jack Truepenny is described as a fellow of 'whorish
      unresisting good-nature.'
239 *Erra pater* a sixteenth-century almanac, *The Pronostycacion for ever of Erra
      Pater, a Jewe born in Jewry, a doctour in Astronomye and Physicke, Profytable
      to kepe the bodye in health*
244 *use to be* (us'd to be Ww)
247 *Cardan* Jerome Cardan (1501–76), Italian mathematician, physician and
      astrologer
248 *Longomontanus* Christian Severin (1562–1647), a Danish astronomer and
      astrologer
249 *chiromancy* palmistry

FORESIGHT

    Ah, Sir Sampson, heaven help your head. This is none of   255
your lucky hour; *nemo omnibus horis sapit*. What, is he
gone, and in contempt of science! Ill stars and unconverted
ignorance attend him.

SCANDAL

    You must excuse his passion, Mr. Foresight, for he has
been heartily vexed. His son is *non compos mentis*, and   260
thereby incapable of making any conveyance in law; so that
all his measures are disappointed.

FORESIGHT

    Ha! say you so?

MRS. FRAIL (*Aside to* MRS. FORESIGHT)

    What, has my sea-lover lost his anchor of hope then?

MRS. FORESIGHT

    O, sister, what will you do with him?   265

MRS. FRAIL

    Do with him? Send him to sea again in the next foul
weather. He's used to an inconstant element, and won't be
surprised to see the tide turned.

FORESIGHT (*Considers*)

    Wherein was I mistaken, not to foresee this?

SCANDAL (*Aside to* MRS. FORESIGHT)

    Madam, you and I can tell him something else that he did   270
not foresee, and more particularly relating to his own fortune.

MRS. FORESIGHT

    What do you mean? I don't understand you.

SCANDAL

    Hush, softly – the pleasures of last night, my dear, too con-
siderable to be forgot so soon.   275

MRS. FORESIGHT

    Last night! And what would your impudence infer from last
night? Last night was like the night before, I think.

SCANDAL

    S'death, do you make no difference between me and your
husband?

MRS. FORESIGHT

    Not much. He's superstitious, and you are mad, in my   280
opinion.

SCANDAL

    You make me mad. You are not serious. Pray recollect
yourself.

---

256 *nemo ... sapit* no one is wise all the time, Pliny, *Nat. Hist.* VII, xl
257 *unconverted* (unconvertible Ww)

MRS. FORESIGHT
O yes, now I remember. You were very impertinent and
impudent, and would have come to bed to me.   285
SCANDAL
And did not?
MRS. FORESIGHT
Did not! With that face can you ask the question?
SCANDAL [*Aside*]
This I have heard of before, but never believed. I have been
told she had that admirable quality of forgetting to a man's
face in the morning that she had lain with him all night, and 290
denying favours with more impudence than she could grant
'em. – Madam, I'm your humble servant and honour you.
– You look pretty well, Mr. Foresight. How did you rest
last night?
FORESIGHT
Truly, Mr. Scandal, I was so taken up with broken dreams 295
and distracted visions that I remember little.
SCANDAL
'Twas a very forgetting night. But would you not talk with
Valentine? Perhaps you may understand him; I'm apt to
believe there is something mysterious in his discourses, and
sometimes rather think him inspired than mad.   300
FORESIGHT
You speak with singular good judgment, Mr. Scandal,
truly. I am inclining to your Turkish opinion in this matter,
and do reverence a man whom the vulgar think mad. Let us
go in to him.
MRS. FRAIL
Sister, do you stay with them; I'll find out my lover and give 305
him his discharge, and come to you. O'my conscience, here
he comes.

Exeunt FORESIGHT, MRS. FORESIGHT, *and* SCANDAL

Enter BEN

BEN
All mad, I think. Flesh, I believe all the calentures of the sea
are come ashore, for my part.
MRS. FRAIL
Mr. Benjamin in choler!   310

---

287 *that face* (what face W2)
291 *denying favours* (denying that she had done favours Ww)
304 *in to him* (to him Ww)
308 *calentures* fevers contracted by sailors in hot climates

BEN

No, I'm pleased well enough, now I have found you. Mess,
I've had such a hurricane upon your account yonder.

MRS. FRAIL

My account! Pray, what's the matter?

BEN

Why, father came and found me squabbling with yon
chitty-faced thing, as he would have me marry; so he asked   315
what was the matter. He asked in a surly sort of a way. (It
seems brother Val is gone mad, and so that put'n into a
passion; but what did I know that, what's that to me?) So
he asked in a surly sort of manner, and gad I answered'n as
surlily. What tho'f he be my father, I an't bound prentice to   320
'en: so faith, I told'n in plain terms, if I were minded to
marry, I'd marry to please myself, not him; and for the
young woman that he provided for me, I thought it more
fitting for her to learn her sampler, and make dirt-pies, than
to look after a husband; for my part I was none of her man.   325
I had another voyage to make, let him take it as he will.

MRS. FRAIL

So then you intend to go to sea again?

BEN

Nay, nay, my mind run upon you, but I would not tell him
so much. So he said he'd make my heart ache, and if so be
that he could get a woman to his mind, he'd marry himself.   330
Gad, says I, an you play the fool and marry at these years,
there's more danger of your head's aching than my heart.
He was woundy angry when I gav'n that wipe. He hadn't a
word to say, and so I left'n and the green girl together.
Mayhap the bee may bite and he'll marry her himself, with   335
all my heart.

MRS. FRAIL

And were you this undutiful and graceless wretch to your
father?

BEN

Then why was he graceless first? If I am undutiful and
graceless, why did he beget me so? I did not get myself.   340

MRS. FRAIL

O impiety! How have I been mistaken! What an inhuman
merciless creature have I set my heart upon? O, I am happy
to have discovered the shelves and quicksands that lurk
beneath that faithless smiling face.

315 *chitty-faced* baby-faced
324 *sampler* ornamental embroidery

BEN

Hey toss! What's the matter now? Why, you ben't angry,   345
be you?

MRS. FRAIL

O, see me no more, for thou wert born amongst rocks,
suckled by whales, cradled in a tempest, and whistled to by
winds; and thou art come forth with fins and scales, and
three rows of teeth, a most outrageous fish of prey.   350

BEN

O Lord, O Lord, she's mad, poor young woman! Love has
turned her senses, her brain is quite overset. Well-a-day,
how shall I do to set her to rights?

MRS. FRAIL

No, no, I am not mad, monster; I am wise enough to find
you out. Hadst thou the impudence to aspire at being a hus-   355
band with that stubborn and disobedient temper? You that
know not how to submit to a father, presume to have a suf-
ficient stock of duty to undergo a wife? I should have been
finely fobbed indeed, very finely fobbed.

BEN

Harkee forsooth; if so be that you are in your right senses,   360
d'ye see, for aught as I perceive I'm like to be finely fobbed
– if I have got anger here upon your account, and you are
tacked about already. What d'ye mean, after all your fair
speeches, and stroking my cheeks, and kissing and hugging,
what, would you sheer off so? Would you, and leave me   365
aground?

MRS. FRAIL

No, I'll leave you adrift, and go which way you will.

BEN

What, are you false-hearted then?

MRS. FRAIL

Only the wind's changed.

BEN

More shame for you – the wind's changed? It's an ill wind   370
blows nobody good. Mayhap I have good riddance on you,
if these be your tricks. What d'ye mean all this while, to
make a fool of me?

MRS. FRAIL

Any fool but a husband.

---

347 *thou wert born* a parody of the imprecations of Dido, Queen of Carthage, on her
       faithless lover, Aeneas (*Aeneid* IV.365f.)
359 *fobbed* cheated
371 *have good* (have a good Ww)
372 *d'ye* (did you Ww)

BEN

Husband! Gad, I would not be your husband, if you would   375
have me, now I know your mind, tho'f you had your weight
in gold and jewels and tho'f I loved you never so well.

MRS. FRAIL

Why, canst thou love, porpoise?

BEN

No matter what I can do. Don't call names – I don't love
you so well as to bear that, whatever I did. I'm glad you   380
show yourself, mistress. Let them marry you as don't know
you. Gad, I know you too well, by sad experience; I believe
he that marries you will go to sea in a hen-pecked frigate. I
believe that, young woman – and mayhap may come to an
anchor at Cuckold's Point; so there's a dash for you, take it   385
as you will. Mayhap you may holla after me when I won't
come to.   *Exit*

MRS. FRAIL

Ha, ha, ha, no doubt on't. – (*Sings*) *My true love is gone to
sea* –

Enter MRS. FORESIGHT

O, sister, had you come a minute sooner, you would have   390
seen the resolution of a lover. Honest Tar and I are parted;
and with the same indifference that we met. O'my life, I am
half vexed at the insensibility of a brute that I despised.

MRS. FORESIGHT

What then, he bore it most heroically?

MRS. FRAIL

Most tyrannically, for you see he has got the start of me;   395
and I, the poor forsaken maid, am left complaining on the
shore. But I'll tell you a hint that he has given me: Sir
Sampson is enraged, and talks desperately of committing
matrimony himself. If he has a mind to throw himself away,
he can't do it more effectually than upon me, if we could   400
bring it about.

MRS. FORESIGHT

O, hang him, old fox, he's too cunning; besides, he hates
both you and me. But I have a project in my head for you,
and I have gone a good way towards it. I have almost made
a bargain with Jeremy, Valentine's man, to sell his master   405
to us.

MRS. FRAIL

Sell him, how?

MRS. FORESIGHT
Valentine raves upon Angelica, and took me for her, and
Jeremy says will take anybody for her that he imposes on
him. Now I have promised him mountains, if in one of his   410
mad fits he will bring you to him in her stead, and get you
married together, and put to bed together; and after con-
summation, girl, there's no revoking. And if he should
recover his senses, he'll be glad at least to make you a good
settlement. – Here they come. Stand aside a little, and tell   415
me how you like the design.

Enter VALENTINE, SCANDAL, FORESIGHT, *and* JEREMY

SCANDAL (*To* JEREMY)
And have you given your master a hint of their plot upon
him?

JEREMY
Yes, sir. He says he'll favour it, and mistake her for
Angelica.   420

SCANDAL
It may make sport.

FORESIGHT
Mercy on us!

VALENTINE
Husht, interrupt me not – I'll whisper prediction to thee,
and thou shalt prophesy. I am Truth, and can teach thy
tongue a new trick. I have told thee what's past, now I tell   425
what's to come. Dost thou know what will happen tomorrow? Answer me not, for I will tell thee. Tomorrow knaves
will thrive through craft, and fools through fortune; and
honesty will go as it did, frost-nipped in a summer suit. Ask
me questions concerning tomorrow.   430

SCANDAL
Ask him, Mr. Foresight.

FORESIGHT
Pray, what will be done at court?

VALENTINE
Scandal will tell you; I am Truth, I never come there.

FORESIGHT
In the city?

VALENTINE
O, prayers will be said in empty churches at the usual   435
hours. Yet you will see such zealous faces behind counters
as if religion were to be sold in every shop. O, things will

421 *make sport* (make us sport Ww)
425 *I tell* (I'll tell you Ww)

go methodically in the city; the clocks will strike twelve at
noon, and the horned herd buzz in the Exchange at two.
Wives and husbands will drive distinct trades, and care and   440
pleasure separately occupy the family. Coffee-houses will
be full of smoke and stratagem, and the cropt prentice, that
sweeps his master's shop in the morning, may ten to one,
dirty his sheets before night. But there are two things that
you will see very strange; which are wanton wives, with   445
their legs at liberty, and tame cuckolds, with chains about
their necks. But hold, I must examine you before I go further; you look suspiciously. Are you a husband?

FORESIGHT

I am married.

VALENTINE

Poor creature! Is your wife of Covent Garden parish?   450

FORESIGHT

No, St. Martin's-in-the-Fields.

VALENTINE

Alas, poor man; his eyes are sunk, and his hands shrivelled;
his legs dwindled, and his back bowed. Pray, pray, for a
metamorphosis. Change thy shape, and shake off age; get
thee Medea's kettle, and be boiled anew; come forth with   455
labouring callous hands, a chine of steel, and Atlas' shoulders. Let Taliacotius trim the calves of twenty chairmen,
and make thee pedestals to stand erect upon and look
matrimony in the face. Ha, ha, ha! That a man should have
a stomach to a wedding supper, when the pigeons ought   460
rather to be laid to his feet, ha, ha, ha.

439 *Exchange* the Royal Exchange, the principal centre for business, in the city close
to the junction of Cornhill and Threadneedle Street. It had been destroyed in the
Great Fire and Charles II had laid the foundation stone for the new building.

440 *Wives and husbands* (Husbands and wives W2)

450 *Covent Garden parish* suggesting either that Foresight's wife is a dissolute
member of high society or a whore. St Martin's is in St. Martin's Lane near
Charing Cross.

455 *Medea's kettle* the cauldron in which the witch Medea prepared the herbs with
which she restored the youth of the aged Aeson

456 *chine* spine
    Atlas the fabled giant who sustained the world on his shoulders

457 *Taliacotius* Gaspar (1549–99), an Italian surgeon famous for his experiments in
skin grafting

460–1 *pigeons ... feet* a restorative for the dying, see Pepys' *Diary*, 19 October 1663,
'The Queen ... was so ill as to be shaved and pidgeons put to her feet, and to
have the extreme unction given her by the priests'

FORESIGHT
His frenzy is very high now, Mr. Scandal.

SCANDAL
I believe it is a spring tide.

FORESIGHT
Very likely truly; you understand these matters. Mr.
Scandal, I shall be very glad to confer with you about these   465
things which he has uttered. His sayings are very mysterious and hieroglyphical.

VALENTINE
O, why would Angelica be absent from my eyes so long?

JEREMY
She's here, sir.

MRS. FORESIGHT
Now, sister.   470

MRS. FRAIL
O Lord, what must I say?

SCANDAL
Humour him, madam, by all means.

VALENTINE
Where is she? O, I see her. She comes, like riches, health,
and liberty at once, to a despairing, starving, and aban-
doned wretch. O welcome, welcome.   475

MRS. FRAIL
How d'ye, sir? Can I serve you?

VALENTINE
Harkee, I have a secret to tell you – Endymion and the
moon shall meet us upon Mount Latmos, and we'll be married in the dead of night – but say not a word. Hymen shall
put his torch into a dark lanthorn, that it may be secret; and   480
Juno shall give her peacock poppy-water, that he may fold
his ogling tail, and Argos's hundred eyes be shut, ha?
Nobody shall know but Jeremy.

MRS. FRAIL
No, no, we'll keep it secret; it shall be done presently.

VALENTINE
The sooner the better. – Jeremy, come hither – closer – that   485
none may overhear us. Jeremy, I can tell you news: Angelica
is turned nun, and I am turning friar, and yet we'll marry

---

477 *Endymion* the shepherd with whom the moon fell in love as he slept on Mount
      Latmos
479–82 *Hymen ... shut* we shall be married in secret. Juno was protectoress of mar-
      riage. Argos was the hundred-eyed watchman she employed to keep Jupiter from
      his mistress Io, but Mercury killed him. His eyes were then placed in the pea-
      cock's tail.

one another in spite of the Pope. Get me a cowl and beads
that I may play my part, for she'll meet me two hours hence
in black and white, and a long veil to cover the project, and 490
we won't see one another's faces till we have done something to be ashamed of; and then we'll blush once for all.

Enter TATTLE *and* ANGELICA

JEREMY

I'll take care, and –

VALENTINE

Whisper.

ANGELICA

Nay, Mr. Tattle, if you make love to me, you spoil my 495
design, for I intended to make you my confidant.

TATTLE

But, madam, to throw away your person, such a person!
and such a fortune, on a madman!

ANGELICA

I never loved him till he was mad; but don't tell anybody
so.   500

SCANDAL

How's this! Tattle making love to Angelica!

TATTLE

Tell, madam! Alas, you don't know me. I have much ado to
tell your ladyship how long I have been in love with you,
but encouraged by the impossibility of Valentine's making
any more addresses to you, I have ventured to declare the 505
very inmost passion of my heart. O, madam, look upon us
both. There you see the ruins of a poor decayed creature,
here, a complete and lively figure, with youth and health,
and all his five senses in perfection, madam, and to all this,
the most passionate lover –   510

ANGELICA

O, fie for shame, hold your tongue; a passionate lover, and
five senses in perfection! When you are as mad as Valentine,
I'll believe you love me, and the maddest shall take me.

VALENTINE

It is enough. Ha! Who's here?

MRS. FRAIL (*To* JEREMY)

O Lord, her coming will spoil all.   515

JEREMY

No, no, madam, he won't know her. If he should I can persuade him.

---

496 *intended* (intend Q3, 4, Ww)
508 *complete and lively* (complete, lively W2)

VALENTINE

Scandal, who are all these? Foreigners? If they are, I'll tell
you what I think. (*Whispers*) Get away all the company but
Angelica, that I may discover my design to her.   520

SCANDAL

I will. I have discovered something of Tattle, that is of a
piece with Mrs. Frail. He courts Angelica, if we could contrive to couple 'em together. Harkee.   *Whispers*

MRS. FORESIGHT

He won't know you, cousin; he knows nobody.

FORESIGHT

But he knows more than anybody. O, niece, he knows   525
things past and to come, and all the profound secrets of
time.

TATTLE

Look you, Mr. Foresight, it is not my way to make many
words of matters, and so I shan't say much, but in short,
d'ye see, I will hold you a hundred pound now that I know   530
more secrets than he.

FORESIGHT

How! I cannot read that knowledge in your face, Mr.
Tattle. Pray, what do you know?

TATTLE

Why d'ye think I'll tell you, sir! Read it in my face? No, sir,
'tis written in my heart. And safer there, sir, than letters   535
writ in juice of lemon, for no fire can fetch it out. I am no
blab, sir.

VALENTINE (*To* SCANDAL)

Acquaint Jeremy with it; he may easily bring it about. They
are welcome, and I'll tell 'em so myself. – What, do you
look strange upon me? Then I must be plain. (*Coming up*   540
to them) I am Truth, and hate an old acquaintance with a
new face.

SCANDAL *goes aside with* JEREMY

TATTLE

Do you know me, Valentine?

VALENTINE

You? Who are you? No, I hope not.

TATTLE

I am Jack Tattle, your friend.   545

VALENTINE

My friend, what to do? I am no married man, and thou
canst not lie with my wife; I am very poor, and thou canst

not borrow money of me; then what employment have I for
a friend?

TATTLE

Hah! A good open speaker, and not to be trusted with a   550
secret.

ANGELICA

Do you know me, Valentine?

VALENTINE

O, very well.

ANGELICA

Who am I?

VALENTINE

You're a woman, one to whom heaven gave beauty when it   555
grafted roses on a briar. You are the reflection of heaven in
a pond, and he that leaps at you is sunk. You are all white,
a sheet of lovely spotless paper, when you first are born; but
you are to be scrawled and blotted by every goose's quill. I
know you; for I loved a woman, and loved her so long that   560
I found out a strange thing: I found out what a woman was
good for.

TATTLE

Aye, prithee, what's that?

VALENTINE

Why, to keep a secret.

TATTLE

O Lord!   565

VALENTINE

O exceeding good to keep a secret: for though she should
tell, yet she is not to be believed.

TATTLE

Hah! good again, faith.

VALENTINE

I would have music. Sing me the song that I like.

SONG
Set by Mr. Finger

I tell thee, Charmion, could I time retrieve,   570
And could again begin to love and live,
To you I should my earliest off'ring give;
    I know my eyes would lead my heart to you,
    And I should all my vows and oaths renew,
    But to be plain, I never would be true.   575

---

569 *Finger* Godfrey Finger (*fl.* 1685–1717), a Moravian composer. He wrote songs
    for Congreve's *The Mourning Bride*.

For by our weak and weary truth, I find,
Love hates to centre in a point assigned,
But runs with joy the circle of the mind.
   Then never let us chain what should be free,
   But for relief of either sex agree,
   Since women love to change, and so do we.

VALENTINE (*Walks musing*)   580
No more, for I am melancholy.

JEREMY (*To* SCANDAL)
I'll do't, sir.

SCANDAL
Mr. Foresight, we had best leave him. He may grow outrageous and do mischief.

FORESIGHT   585
I will be directed by you.

JEREMY (*To* MRS. FRAIL)
You'll meet, madam, I'll take care everything shall be ready.

MRS. FRAIL
Thou shalt do what thou wilt, have what thou wilt; in short, I will deny thee nothing.

TATTLE (*To* ANGELICA)
Madam, shall I wait upon you?   590

ANGELICA
No, I'll stay with him; Mr. Scandal will protect me. Aunt, Mr. Tattle desires you would give him leave to wait on you.

TATTLE [*Aside*]
Pox on't, there's no coming off, now she has said that. – Madam, will you do me the honour?

MRS. FORESIGHT
Mr. Tattle might have used less ceremony.   595

Exeunt FORESIGHT, MRS. FORESIGHT, TATTLE, MRS. FRAIL

SCANDAL
Jeremy, follow Tattle.

Exit JEREMY

ANGELICA
Mr. Scandal, I only stay till my maid comes, and because I had a mind to be rid of Mr. Tattle.

SCANDAL
Madam, I am very glad that I overheard a better reason, which you gave to Mr. Tattle; for his impertinence forced

590 *have what thou wilt* (om. Ww)

you to acknowledge a kindness for Valentine, which you   600
denied to all his sufferings and my solicitations. So I'll leave
him to make use of the discovery, and your ladyship to the
free confession of your inclinations.

ANGELICA

O heavens! You won't leave me alone with a madman?   605

SCANDAL

No, madam; I only leave a madman to his remedy.   *Exit*

VALENTINE

Madam, you need not be very much afraid, for I fancy I
begin to come to myself.

ANGELICA (*Aside*)

Aye, but if I don't fit you, I'll be hanged.

VALENTINE

You see what disguises love makes us put on. Gods have   610
been in counterfeited shapes for the same reason, and the
divine part of me, my mind, has worn this mask of madness, and this motley livery, only as the slave of love, and
menial creature of your beauty.

ANGELICA

Mercy on me, how he talks! Poor Valentine!   615

VALENTINE

Nay, faith, now let us understand one another, hypocrisy
apart. The comedy draws toward an end, and let us think
of leaving acting and be ourselves; and since you have loved
me, you must own I have at length deserved you should
confess it.

ANGELICA (*Sighs*)   620

I would I had loved you, for heaven knows I pity you; and
could I have foreseen the sad effects, I would have striven;
but that's too late.

VALENTINE

What sad effects? What's too late? My seeming madness
has deceived my father, and procured me time to think of
means to reconcile me to him and preserve the right of my   625
inheritance to his estate, which otherwise by articles I must
this morning have resigned: and this I had informed you of
today, but you were gone before I knew you had been here.

ANGELICA

How! I thought your love of me had caused this transport   630
in your soul, which, it seems, you only counterfeited for
mercenary ends and sordid interest.

---

610 *fit* punish, trick
623 *sad effects* (bad effects Q3, 4, Ww)
632–3 *for mercenary* (for by, mercenary Q1, 2; for by mercenary Q3, 4, W1)

VALENTINE

Nay, now you do me wrong; for if any interest was considered, it was yours, since I thought I wanted more than
love to make me worthy of you.

ANGELICA   635

Then you thought me mercenary. – But how am I deluded
by this interval of sense, to reason with a madman?

VALENTINE

O, 'tis barbarous to misunderstand me longer.

Enter JEREMY

ANGELICA

O, here's a reasonable creature. – Sure he will not have the
impudence to persevere. – Come, Jeremy, acknowledge
your trick, and confess your master's madness counterfeit.   640

JEREMY

Counterfeit, madam! I'll maintain him to be as absolutely
and substantially mad as any freeholder in Bethlehem; nay,
he's as mad as any projector, fanatic, chemist, lover, or poet
in Europe.

VALENTINE   645

Sirrah, you lie; I am not mad.

ANGELICA

Ha, ha, ha, you see he denies it.

JEREMY

O Lord, madam, did you ever know any madman mad
enough to own it?

VALENTINE   650

Sot, can't you apprehend?

ANGELICA

Why, he talked very sensibly just now.

JEREMY

Yes, madam, he has intervals: but you see he begins to look
wild again now.

VALENTINE

Why, you thick-skulled rascal, I tell you the farce is done,
and I will be mad no longer.   *Beats him*

ANGELICA   655

Ha, ha, ha, is he mad, or no, Jeremy?

JEREMY

Partly, I think, for he does not know his mind two hours.
I'm sure I left him just now in a humour to be mad, and I

---

644 *Bethlehem* St. Mary of Bethlehem, the lunatic asylum (Bedlam)
658 *his mind* (his own mind Ww)
659 *a humour* (the humour Ww)

think I have not found him very quiet at this present. (*One knocks*) Who's there?

VALENTINE   660

Go see, you sot. – I'm very glad that I can move your mirth, though not your compassion.

Exit JEREMY

ANGELICA

I did not think you had apprehension enough to be exceptious: but madmen show themselves most by overpretending to a sound understanding, as drunken men do by over-acting sobriety. I was half inclining to believe you, till   665
I accidentally touched upon your tender part; but now you have restored me to my former opinion and compassion.

Enter JEREMY

JEREMY

Sir, your father has sent to know if you are any better yet. Will you please to be mad, sir, or how?

VALENTINE   670

Stupidity! You know the penalty of all I'm worth must pay for the confession of my senses; I'm mad, and will be mad to everybody but this lady.

JEREMY

So, just the very backside of Truth. But lying is a figure in speech that interlards the greatest part of my conversation.
– Madam, your ladyship's woman.   *Goes to the door*   675

Enter JENNY

ANGELICA

Well, have you been there? Come hither.

JENNY

Yes, madam. (*Aside to* ANGELICA) Sir Sampson will wait upon you presently.

VALENTINE

You are not leaving me in this uncertainty?   680

ANGELICA

Would anything but a madman complain of uncertainty? Uncertainty and expectation are the joys of life. Security is an insipid thing, and the overtaking and possessing of a wish discovers the folly of the chase. Never let us know one another better; for the pleasure of a masquerade is done when we come to show faces. But I'll tell you two things   685

663 s.d. *Exit* JEREMY (om. Ww)
669 s.d. *Enter* JEREMY (om. Ww)
687 *show faces* (show our faces Ww)

before I leave you: I am not the fool you take me for; and
you are mad and don't know it.

Exeunt ANGELICA *and* JENNY

VALENTINE
From a riddle you can expect nothing but a riddle. There's
my instruction, and the moral of my lesson.

Re-enter JEREMY   690

JEREMY
What, is the lady gone again, sir? I hope you understood
one another before she went?
VALENTINE
Understood! She is harder to be understood than a piece of
Egyptian antiquity, or an Irish manuscript; you may pore
till you spoil your eyes, and not improve your knowledge.
JEREMY   695
I have heard 'em say, sir, they read hard Hebrew books
backwards; maybe you begin to read at the wrong end.
VALENTINE
They say so of a witch's prayer, and dreams and Dutch
almanacs are to be understood by contraries. But there's
regularity and method in that; she is a medal without a
reverse or inscription, for indifference has both sides alike. 700
Yet while she does not seem to hate me, I will pursue her,
and know her if it be possible, in spite of the opinion of my
satirical friend, Scandal, who says
      That women are like tricks by sleight of hand,
      Which, to admire, we should not understand.   705

Exeunt

Act V

A room in FORESIGHT'*s house*

Enter ANGELICA *and* JENNY

ANGELICA
Where is Sir Sampson? Did you not tell me he would be
here before me?

JENNY
He's at the great glass in the dining room, madam, setting
his cravat and wig.

ANGELICA
How! I'm glad on't. If he has a mind I should like him, it's   5
a sign he likes me; and that's more than half my design.

JENNY
I hear him, madam.

ANGELICA
Leave me, and, d'ye hear, if Valentine should come, or
send, I am not to be spoken with.

Exit JENNY

Enter SIR SAMPSON

SIR SAMPSON
I have not been honoured with the commands of a fair lady   10
a great while – odd, madam, you have revived me – not
since I was five and thirty.

ANGELICA
Why, you have no great reason to complain, Sir Sampson;
that is not long ago.

SIR SAMPSON
Zooks, but it is, madam, a very great while; to a man that   15
admires a fine woman as much as I do.

ANGELICA
You're an absolute courtier, Sir Sampson.

SIR SAMPSON
Not at all, madam; odsbud, you wrong me: I am not so old,
neither, to be a bare courtier, only a man of words. Odd, I
have warm blood about me yet; I can serve a lady any way.   20
Come, come, let me tell you, you women think a man old
too soon, faith and troth you do. Come, don't despise fifty;
odd, fifty, in a hale constitution, is no such contemptible
age.

20 *I can* (and can Q3, 4, Ww)

ANGELICA

Fifty a contemptible age! Not at all, a very fashionable age   25
I think. I assure you I know very considerable beaux that
set a good face upon fifty. Fifty! I have seen fifty in a side
box, by candle-light, out-blossom five and twenty.

SIR SAMPSON

O pox, outsides, outsides, a pize take 'em, mere outsides.
Hang your side-box beaux; no, I'm none of those, none of   30
your forced trees, that pretend to blossom in the fall, and
bud when they should bring forth fruit. I am of a long-lived
race, and inherit vigour; none of my family married till fifty,
yet they begot sons and daughters till fourscore. I am of
your patriarchs, I, a branch of one of your antediluvian   35
families, fellows that the flood could not wash away. Well,
madam, what are your commands? Has any young rogue
affronted you, and shall I cut his throat? or –

ANGELICA

No, Sir Sampson, I have no quarrel upon my hands; I have
more occasion for your conduct than your courage at this   40
time. To tell you the truth, I'm weary of living single, and
want a husband.

SIR SAMPSON

Odsbud, and 'tis pity you should. (Aside) Odd, would she
would like me; then I should hamper my young rogues;
odd, would she would; faith and troth, she's devilish hand-   45
some. – Madam, you deserve a good husband, and 'twere
pity you should be thrown away upon any of these young
idle rogues about the town. Odd, there's ne'er a young
fellow worth hanging – that is a very young fellow. Pize on
'em, they never think beforehand of anything; and if they   50
commit matrimony, 'tis as they commit murder, out of a
frolic; and are ready to hang themselves, or to be hanged by
the law, the next morning. Odso, have a care, madam.

ANGELICA

Therefore I ask your advice, Sir Sampson: I have fortune
enough to make any man easy that I can like; if there were   55
such a thing as a young, agreeable man, with a reasonable
stock of good nature and sense – for I would neither have
an absolute wit, nor a fool.

SIR SAMPSON

Odd, you are hard to please, madam; to find a young fellow

29 O pox (om. Ww)

33 family (ancestors Ww)

46–7 'twere pity ('twere a pity Q4)

49 that is (that's Q2)

that is neither a wit in his own eye, nor a fool in the eye of   60
the world, is a very hard task. But, faith and troth, you
speak very discreetly, for I hate both a wit and a fool.

ANGELICA
She that marries a fool, Sir Sampson, commits the reputation of her honesty or understanding to the censure of the
world; and she that marries a very witty man submits both   65
to the severity and insolent conduct of her husband. I
should like a man of wit for a lover, because I would have
such an one in my power; but I would no more be his wife
than his enemy; for his malice is not a more terrible consequence of his aversion, than his jealousy is of his love.   70

SIR SAMPSON
None of old Foresight's sibyls ever uttered such a truth.
Odsbud, you have won my heart; I hate a wit – I had a son
that was spoiled among 'em; a good, hopeful lad, till he
learned to be a wit – and might have risen in the state. But,
a pox on't, his wit run him out of his money, and now his   75
poverty has run him out of his wits.

ANGELICA
Sir Sampson, as your friend, I must tell you, you are very
much abused in that matter; he's no more mad than you
are.

SIR SAMPSON
How, madam! Would I could prove it.   80

ANGELICA
I can tell you how that may be done. – But it is a thing that
would make me appear to be too much concerned in your
affairs.

SIR SAMPSON (*Aside*)
Odsbud, I believe she likes me. – Ah, madam, all my affairs
are scarce worthy to be laid at your feet; and I wish,   85
madam, they stood in a better posture, that I might make a
more becoming offer to a lady of your incomparable beauty
and merit. If I had Peru in one hand and Mexico in t'other,
and the Eastern Empire under my feet, it would make me
only a more glorious victim to be offered at the shrine of   90
your beauty.

ANGELICA
Bless me, Sir Sampson, what's the matter?

63–5 *commits* (forfeits Ww) *to the censure of the world* (om. Ww)
65 *submits both* (is a slave Ww)
86 *stood* (were Ww)

SIR SAMPSON
  Odd, madam, I love you, and if you would take my advice
  in a husband –

ANGELICA
  Hold, hold, Sir Sampson. I asked your advice for a hus-   95
  band, and you are giving me your consent. I was indeed
  thinking to propose something like it in a jest, to satisfy you
  about Valentine: for if a match were seemingly carried on
  between you and me, it would oblige him to throw off his
  disguise of madness in apprehension of losing me, for you   100
  know he has long pretended a passion for me.

SIR SAMPSON
  Gadzooks, a most ingenious contrivance – if we were to go
  through with it. But why must the match only be seemingly
  carried on? Odd, let it be a real contract.

ANGELICA
  O fie, Sir Sampson, what would the world say?   105

SIR SAMPSON
  Say, they would say, you were a wise woman, and I a happy
  man. Odd, madam, I'll love you as long as I live, and leave
  you a good jointure when I die.

ANGELICA
  Aye, but that is not in your power, Sir Sampson; for when
  Valentine confesses himself in his senses, he must make   110
  over his inheritance to his younger brother.

SIR SAMPSON
  Odd, you're cunning, a wary baggage! Faith and troth, I
  like you the better. But, I warrant you, I have a proviso in
  the obligation in favour of myself. Body o'me, I have a trick
  to turn the settlement upon the issue male of our two   115
  bodies begotten. Odsbud, let us find children, and I'll find
  an estate.

ANGELICA
  Will you? Well, do you find the estate, and leave the t'other
  to me –

SIR SAMPSON
  O rogue! But I'll trust you. And will you consent? Is it a   120
  match then?

ANGELICA
  Let me consult my lawyer concerning this obligation; and if
  I find what you propose practicable, I'll give you my
  answer.

97 *a jest* (jest Q3, 4, Ww)
118 *the t'other* (the other W2)

SIR SAMPSON

    With all my heart. Come in with me, and I'll lend you the   125
bond. You shall consult your lawyer, and I'll consult a
parson. Odzooks, I'm a young man; odzooks, I'm a young
man, and I'll make it appear. – Odd, you're devilish handsome; faith and troth, you're very handsome, and I'm very
young, and very lusty. Odsbud, hussy, you know how to   130
choose, and so do I. Odd, I think we are very well met. Give
me your hand; odd, let me kiss it; 'tis as warm and as soft
– as what? – odd, as t'other hand – give me t'other hand,
and I'll mumble 'em, and kiss 'em till they melt in my
mouth.   135

ANGELICA

    Hold, Sir Sampson, you're profuse of your vigour before
your time: you'll spend your estate before you come to it.

SIR SAMPSON

    No, no, only give you a rent-roll of my possessions – ah
baggage! – I warrant you, for little Sampson. Odd,
Sampson's a very good name for an able fellow: your   140
Sampsons were strong dogs from the beginning.

ANGELICA

    Have a care, and don't over-act your part. If you remem-
ber, the strongest Sampson of your name pulled an old
house over his head at last.

SIR SAMPSON

    Say you so, hussy? Come, let's go then. Odd, I long to be   145
pulling down too, come away. Odso, here's somebody
coming.

Exeunt

Enter TATTLE *and* JEREMY

TATTLE

    Is not that she, gone out just now?

JEREMY

    Aye, sir, she's just going to the place of appointment. Ah,
sir, if you are not very faithful and close in this business,   150
you'll certainly be the death of a person that has a most
extraordinary passion for your honour's service.

TATTLE

    Aye, who's that?

143 *the strongest ... name* (Sampson, the strongest of the name Ww)
143–4 *old house* 'I have brought an old House upon my Head, Intail'd Cuckoldom
    upon my self', Sir Cautious in Aphra Behn *The Lucky Chance* V.vii.
146 *pulling down* (pulling Ww)

JEREMY

    Even my unworthy self, sir. Sir, I have had an appetite to be
    fed with your commands a great while; and now, sir, my   155
    former master having much troubled the fountain of his
    understanding, it is a very plausible occasion for me to
    quench my thirst at the spring of your bounty. I thought I
    could not recommend myself better to you, sir, than by the
    delivery of a great beauty and fortune into your arms,   160
    whom I have heard you sigh for.

TATTLE

    I'll make thy fortune; say no more. Thou art a pretty fellow,
    and canst carry a message to a lady in a pretty soft kind of
    phrase, and with a good persuading accent.

JEREMY

    Sir, I have the seeds of rhetoric and oratory in my head – I   165
    have been at Cambridge.

TATTLE

    Aye, 'tis well enough for a servant to be bred at an univer-
    sity, but the education is a little too pedantic for a gentle-
    man. I hope you are secret in your nature, private, close,
    ha?   170

JEREMY

    O, sir, for that, sir, 'tis my chief talent; I'm as secret as the
    head of Nilus.

TATTLE

    Aye? Who's he, though? A Privy Counsellor?

JEREMY (*Aside*)

    O ignorance! – A cunning Egyptian, sir, that with his arms
    would overrun the country, yet nobody could ever find out   175
    his headquarters.

TATTLE

    Close dog! A good whoremaster, I warrant him. – The time
    draws nigh, Jeremy. Angelica will be veiled like a nun, and
    I must be hooded like a friar, ha, Jeremy?

JEREMY

    Aye, sir, hooded like a hawk, to seize at first sight upon the   180
    quarry. It is the whim of my master's madness to be so
    dressed; and she is so in love with him, she'll comply with
    anything to please him. Poor lady, I'm sure she'll have
    reason to pray for me, when she finds what a happy

---

172 *head of Nilus* Sir Peter Wyche had published *A short relation of the River Nile*
    (1669) translated from the Portuguese on the discovery of the source of the Blue
    Nile. The source of the White Nile was not discovered until the nineteenth cen-
    tury.

exchange she has made between a madman and so accom-　185
plished a gentleman.

TATTLE

Aye, faith, so she will, Jeremy: you're a good friend to her,
poor creature. I swear I do it hardly so much in consideration of myself, as compassion to her.

JEREMY

'Tis an act of charity, sir, to save a fine woman with 30,000　190
pound from throwing herself away.

TATTLE

So 'tis, faith. I might have saved several others in my time;
but, egad, I could never find in my heart to marry anybody
before.

JEREMY

Well, sir, I'll go and tell her my master's coming; and meet　195
you in half a quarter of an hour, with your disguise, at your
own lodgings. You must talk a little madly; she won't distinguish the tone of your voice.

TATTLE

No, no, let me alone for a counterfeit; I'll be ready for you.

Enter MISS PRUE

MISS PRUE

O, Mr. Tattle, are you here! I'm glad I have found you; I　200
have been looking up and down for you like anything, till
I'm as tired as anything in the world.

TATTLE (*Aside*)

O pox, how shall I get rid of this foolish girl?

MISS PRUE

O, I have pure news; I can tell you pure news. I must not
marry the seaman now; my father says so. Why won't you　205
be my husband? You say you love me, and you won't be my
husband. And I know you may be my husband now if you
please.

TATTLE

O fie, miss; who told you so, child?

MISS PRUE

Why, my father. I told him that you loved me.　　　　　210

TATTLE

O fie, miss, why did you do so? And who told you so, child?

MISS PRUE

Who? Why, you did; did not you?

TATTLE

O pox, that was yesterday, miss; that was a great while ago,
child. I have been asleep since; slept a whole night, and did
not so much as dream of the matter.　　　　　　　　　215

MISS PRUE

Pshaw. O, but I dreamt that it was so, though.

TATTLE

Aye, but your father will tell you that dreams come by contraries, child. O fie; what, we must not love one another
now; pshaw, that would be a foolish thing indeed. Fie, fie,
you're a woman now, and must think of a new man every   220
morning, and forget him every night. No, no, to marry is to
be a child again, and play with the same rattle always. O
fie, marrying is a paw thing.

MISS PRUE

Well, but don't you love me as well as you did last night,
then?   225

TATTLE

No, no, child, you would not have me.

MISS PRUE

No? Yes, but I would, though.

TATTLE

Pshaw, but I tell you, you would not. You forget you're a
woman and don't know your own mind.

MISS PRUE

But here's my father, and he knows my mind.   230

Enter FORESIGHT

FORESIGHT

O, Mr. Tattle, your servant. You are a close man, but
methinks your love to my daughter was a secret I might
have been trusted with – or had you a mind to try if I could
discover it by my art. Hum, ha! I think there is something
in your physiognomy that has a resemblance of her; and the   235
girl is like me.

TATTLE

And so you would infer that you and I are alike. (*Aside*)
What does the old prig mean? I'll banter him, and laugh at
him, and leave him. – I fancy you have a wrong notion of
faces.   240

FORESIGHT

How? What? A wrong notion! How so?

TATTLE

In the way of art. I have some taking features, not obvious
to vulgar eyes, that are indications of a sudden turn of good
fortune in the lottery of wives, and promise a great beauty
and great fortune reserved alone for me, by a private   245

intrigue of destiny, kept secret from the piercing eye of per-
spicuity, from all astrologers and the stars themselves.

FORESIGHT

How! I will make it appear that what you say is impossible.

TATTLE

Sir, I beg your pardon; I'm in haste –

FORESIGHT

For what?   250

TATTLE

To be married, sir, married.

FORESIGHT

Aye, but pray take me along with you, sir –

TATTLE

No, sir; 'tis to be done privately. I never make confidants.

FORESIGHT

Well; but my consent, I mean. You won't marry my daughter without my consent?   255

TATTLE

Who, I, sir? I'm an absolute stranger to you and your
daughter, sir.

FORESIGHT

Hey day! What time of the moon is this?

TATTLE

Very true, sir, and desire to continue so. I have no more
love for your daughter than I have likeness of you; and I   260
have a secret in my heart, which you would be glad to
know, and shan't know; and yet you shall know it too, and
be sorry for't afterwards. I'd have you to know, sir, that I
am as knowing as the stars, and as secret as the night. And
I'm going to be married just now, yet did not know of it   265
half an hour ago; and the lady stays for me, and does not
know of it yet. There's a mystery for you. – I know you love
to untie difficulties. Or if you can't solve this, stay here a
quarter of an hour, and I'll come and explain it to you.

                                                          Exit

MISS PRUE

O, father, why will you let him go? Won't you make him   270
be my husband?

FORESIGHT

Mercy on us, what do these lunacies portend? Alas! he's
mad, child, stark wild.

MISS PRUE

What, and must not I have e'er a husband then? What,

270–1 *him be* (him to be Q3, 4, Ww)

must I go to bed to nurse again, and be a child as long as 275
she's an old woman? Indeed, but I won't: for now my mind
is set upon a man, I will have a man some way or other. O!
methinks I'm sick when I think of a man; and if I can't have
one, I would go to sleep all my life, for when I'm awake, it
makes me wish and long, and I don't know for what – and 280
I'd rather be always asleeping, than sick with thinking.

FORESIGHT
O fearful! I think the girl's influenced too. – Hussy, you
shall have a rod.

MISS PRUE
A fiddle of a rod, I'll have a husband; and if you won't get
me one, I'll get one for myself: I'll marry our Robin, the 285
butler. He says he loves me, and he's a handsome man, and
shall be my husband. I warrant he'll be my husband and
thank me too, for he told me so.

Enter SCANDAL, MRS. FORESIGHT, *and* NURSE

FORESIGHT
Did he so – I'll dispatch him for't presently. Rogue! – O,
nurse, come hither. 290

NURSE
What is your worship's pleasure?

FORESIGHT
Here, take your young mistress, and lock her up presently,
till further orders from me. Not a word, hussy; do what I
bid you; no reply, away. And bid Robin make ready to give
an account of his plate and linen; d'ye hear, be gone when 295
I bid you.

Exeunt NURSE *and* MISS PRUE

MRS. FORESIGHT
What's the matter, husband?

FORESIGHT
'Tis not convenient to tell you now. – Mr. Scandal, heaven
keep us all in our senses; I fear there is a contagious frenzy
abroad. How does Valentine? 300

SCANDAL
O, I hope he will do well again. I have a message from him
to your niece Angelica.

---

281 *always asleeping* (always asleep Q3, 4, Ww)
296 s.d. *Exeunt* NURSE *and* MISS PRUE (om. Ww, but add at the end of the scene;
    Nurse, why are you not gone?)

FORESIGHT

I think she has not returned since she went abroad with Sir
Sampson.

Enter BEN

MRS. FORESIGHT

Here's Mr. Benjamin, he can tell us if his father be come   305
home.

BEN

Who, father? Aye he's come home with a vengeance.

MRS. FORESIGHT

Why, what's the matter?

BEN

Matter! Why, he's mad.

FORESIGHT

Mercy on us, I was afraid of this.   310

BEN

And there's the handsome young woman, she, as they say,
brother Val went mad for; she's mad too, I think.

FORESIGHT

O my poor niece, my poor niece, is she gone too? Well, I
shall run mad next.

MRS. FORESIGHT

Well, but how mad? How d'ye mean?   315

BEN

Nay, I'll give you leave to guess. I'll undertake to make a
voyage to Antigua; no, hold, I mayn't say so neither – but
I'll sail as far as Leghorn and back again, before you shall
guess at the matter, and do nothing else; mess, you may
take in all the points of the compass, and not hit right.   320

MRS. FORESIGHT

Your experiment will take up a little too much time.

BEN

Why, then, I'll tell you: there's a new wedding upon the
stocks, and they two are a-going to be married to rights.

SCANDAL

Who?

BEN

Why, father and – the young woman. I can't hit of her   325
name.

SCANDAL

Angelica?

BEN

Aye, the same.

317 *no, hold, I* (no, I W2)

MRS. FORESIGHT
   Sir Sampson and Angelica, impossible!

BEN
   That may be, but I'm sure it is as I tell you.   330

SCANDAL
   S'death, it's a jest. I can't believe it.

BEN
   Look you, friend, it's nothing to me whether you believe it
   or no. What I say is true; d'ye see, they are married, or just
   going to be married, I know not which.

FORESIGHT
   Well, but they are not mad, that is, not lunatic?   335

BEN
   I don't know what you may call madness, but she's mad for
   a husband, and he's horn-mad, I think, or they'd ne'er
   make a match together. – Here they come.

       Enter SIR SAMPSON, ANGELICA, *with* BUCKRAM

SIR SAMPSON
   Where is this old soothsayer, this uncle of mine elect? Aha,
   old Foresight, uncle Foresight, wish me joy, uncle   340
   Foresight, double joy, both as uncle and astrologer; here's
   a conjunction that was not foretold in all your Ephemeris.
   The brightest star in the blue firmament – is shot from
   above, in a jelly of love, and so forth; and I'm lord of the
   ascendant. Odd, you're an old fellow, Foresight, uncle I   345
   mean, a very old fellow, uncle Foresight; and yet you shall
   live to dance at my wedding; faith and troth, you shall.
   Odd, we'll have the music of the spheres for thee, old Lilly,
   that we will, and thou shalt lead up a dance in *via lactea*.

FORESIGHT
   I'm thunderstruck! You are not married to my niece?   350

SIR SAMPSON
   Not absolutely married, uncle, but very near it; within a
   kiss of the matter, as you see.   *Kisses* ANGELICA

ANGELICA
   'Tis very true indeed, uncle; I hope you'll be my father, and
   give me.

SIR SAMPSON
   That he shall, or I'll burn his globes. Body o'me, he shall be 355
   thy father, I'll make him thy father, and thou shalt make me

---

343–4 *brightest star ... jelly of love* The star is Venus, the jelly Dryden's, from
   Tyrannic Love IV.i: 'And drop from above/In a jelly of love!' The play had been
   revived at the Theatre Royal 1694.
349 *via lactea* the Milky Way

a father, and I'll make thee a mother, and we'll beget sons
and daughters enough to put the weekly bills out of countenance.

SCANDAL

Death and hell! Where's Valentine?   *Exit*   360

MRS. FORESIGHT

This is so surprising –

SIR SAMPSON

How! What does my aunt say? Surprising, aunt? Not at all,
for a young couple to make a match in winter. Not at all –
it's a plot to undermine cold weather, and destroy that
usurper of a bed called a warming pan.   365

MRS. FORESIGHT

I'm glad to hear you have so much fire in you, Sir Sampson.

BEN

Mess, I fear his fire's little better than tinder; mayhap it will
only serve to light up a match for somebody else. The
young woman's a handsome young woman, I can't deny it;
but, father, if I might be your pilot in this case, you should   370
not marry her. It's just the same thing as if so be you should
sail so far as the Straits without provision.

SIR SAMPSON

Who gave you authority to speak, sirrah? To your element,
fish; be mute, fish, and to sea; rule your helm, sirrah, don't
direct me.   375

BEN

Well, well, take you care of your own helm, or you mayn't
keep your own vessel steady.

SIR SAMPSON

Why, you impudent tarpaulin! Sirrah, do you bring your
forecastle jests upon your father? But I shall be even with
you: I won't give you a groat. Mr. Buckram, is the con-   380
veyance so worded that nothing can possibly descend to
this scoundrel? I would not so much as have him have the
prospect of an estate, though there were no way to come to
it, but by the Northeast Passage.

BUCKRAM

Sir, it is drawn according to your directions; there is not the   385
least cranny of the law unstopt.

BEN

Lawyer, I believe there's many a cranny and leak unstopt in

---

358 *weekly bills* the 'bills of mortality' listing those who had died
372 *Straits* of Gibraltar
376 *own* (new Q3, 4, Ww)
384 *Northeast Passage* the impossible route north of Russia to the east

your conscience. If so be that one had a pump to your
bosom, I believe we should discover a foul hold. They say
a witch will sail in a sieve, but I believe the devil would not   390
venture aboard o'your conscience. And that's for you.

SIR SAMPSON
Hold your tongue, sirrah. How now, who's there?

Enter TATTLE *and* MRS. FRAIL

MRS. FRAIL
O, sister, the most unlucky accident!

MRS. FORESIGHT
What's the matter?

TATTLE
O, the two most unfortunate poor creatures in the world   395
we are.

FORESIGHT
Bless us! How so?

MRS. FRAIL
Ah, Mr. Tattle and I, poor Mr. Tattle and I are – I can't
speak it out.

TATTLE
Nor I – but poor Mrs. Frail and I are –   400

MRS. FRAIL
Married.

MRS. FORESIGHT
Married! How?

TATTLE
Suddenly – before we knew where we were – that villain
Jeremy, by the help of disguises, tricked us into one
another.   405

FORESIGHT
Why, you told me just now you went hence in haste to be
married.

ANGELICA
But I believe Mr. Tattle meant the favour to me; I thank
him.

TATTLE
I did; as I hope to be saved, madam, my intentions were   410
good. But this is the most cruel thing, to marry one does not
know how, nor why, nor wherefore. The devil take me if
ever I was so much concerned at anything in my life.

392   *there*? (here? Ww)
393   *sister* (sir Q4)
400   *but poor* (poor Ww)

ANGELICA
'Tis very unhappy, if you don't care for one another.

TATTLE
The least in the world – that is for my part; I speak for   415
myself. Gad, I never had the least thought of serious kindness; I never liked anybody less in my life. Poor woman!
Gad, I'm sorry for her too, for I have no reason to hate her
neither; but I believe I shall lead her a damned sort of life.

MRS. FORESIGHT (*Aside to* MRS. FRAIL)
He's better than no husband at all, though he's a coxcomb.   420

MRS. FRAIL (*To her*)
Aye, aye, it's well it's no worse. – Nay, for my part I always
despised Mr. Tattle of all things; nothing but his being my
husband could have made me like him less.

TATTLE
Look you there, I thought as much. Pox on't, I wish we
could keep it secret. Why, I don't believe any of this   425
company would speak of it.

MRS. FRAIL
But, my dear, that's impossible; the parson and that rogue
Jeremy will publish it.

TATTLE
Aye, my dear; so they will, as you say.

ANGELICA
O, you'll agree very well in a little time; custom will make   430
it easy to you.

TATTLE
Easy! Pox on't, I don't believe I shall sleep tonight.

SIR SAMPSON
Sleep, quotha! No! Why you would not sleep o'your wedding night? I'm an older fellow than you, and don't mean
to sleep.   435

BEN
Why, there's another match now, as tho'f a couple of pri-
vateers were looking for a prize, and should fall foul of one
another. I'm sorry for the young man with all my heart.
Look you, friend, if I may advise you, when she's going –
for that you must expect, I have experience of her – when   440
she's going, let her go. For no matrimony is tough enough
to hold her, and if she can't drag her anchor along with her,
she'll break her cable, I can tell you that. Who's here? The
madman?

Enter VALENTINE *dressed,* SCANDAL, *and* JEREMY

VALENTINE
No, here's the fool; and if occasion be, I'll give it under my   445
hand.

SIR SAMPSON
  How now?
VALENTINE
  Sir, I'm come to acknowledge my errors, and ask your
  pardon.
SIR SAMPSON
  What, have you found your senses at last then? In good   450
  time, sir.
VALENTINE
  You were abused, sir; I never was distracted.
FORESIGHT
  How! Not mad! Mr. Scandal?
SCANDAL
  No really, sir; I'm his witness; it was all counterfeit.
VALENTINE
  I thought I had reasons. But it was a poor contrivance; the   455
  effect has shown it such.
SIR SAMPSON
  Contrivance, what, to cheat me? To cheat your father!
  Sirrah, could you hope to prosper?
VALENTINE
  Indeed, I thought, sir, when the father endeavoured to undo
  the son, it was a reasonable return of nature.   460
SIR SAMPSON
  Very good, sir. – Mr. Buckram, are you ready? – Come, sir,
  will you sign and seal?
VALENTINE
  If you please, sir; but first I would ask this lady one ques-
  tion.
SIR SAMPSON
  Sir, you must ask my leave first. That lady, no, sir; you shall   465
  ask that lady no questions, till you have asked her blessing,
  sir; that lady is to be my wife.
VALENTINE
  I have heard as much, sir; but I would have it from her own
  mouth.
SIR SAMPSON
  That's as much as to say I lie, sir, and you don't believe   470
  what I say.
VALENTINE
  Pardon me, sir. But I reflect that I very lately counterfeited
  madness; I don't know but the frolic may go round.

465 *my leave* (me leave Q3, 4, Ww)

SIR SAMPSON
   Come, chuck, satisfy him, answer him. – Come, come, Mr.
   Buckram, the pen and ink.   475
BUCKRAM
   Here it is, sir, with the deed; all is ready.

                 VALENTINE *goes to* ANGELICA

ANGELICA
   'Tis true, you have a great while pretended love to me; nay,
   what if you were sincere? Still you must pardon me, if I
   think my own inclinations have a better right to dispose of
   my person, than yours.   480
SIR SAMPSON
   Are you answered now, sir?
VALENTINE
   Yes, sir.
SIR SAMPSON
   Where's your plot, sir, and your contrivance now, sir? Will
   you sign, sir? Come, will you sign and seal?
VALENTINE
   With all my heart, sir.   485
SCANDAL
   S'death, you are not mad, indeed, to ruin yourself?
VALENTINE
   I have been disappointed of my only hope; and he that loses
   hope may part with anything. I never valued fortune, but as
   it was subservient to my pleasure; and my only pleasure
   was to please this lady. I have made many vain attempts,   490
   and find at last that nothing but my ruin can effect it:
   which, for that reason, I will sign to – give me the paper.
ANGELICA (*Aside*)
   Generous Valentine!
BUCKRAM
   Here is the deed, sir.
VALENTINE
   But where is the bond by which I am obliged to sign this?   495
BUCKRAM
   Sir Sampson, you have it.
ANGELICA
   No, I have it; and I'll use it as I would everything that is an
   enemy to Valentine.   *Tears the paper*
SIR SAMPSON
   How now!

474 *Come, come, Mr.* (Come, Mr. W2)

VALENTINE

Ha!   500

ANGELICA (*To* VALENTINE)

Had I the world to give you, it could not make me worthy
of so generous and faithful a passion: here's my hand, my
heart was always yours, and struggled very hard to make
this utmost trial of your virtue.

VALENTINE

Between pleasure and amazement, I am lost – but on my   505
knees I take the blessing.

SIR SAMPSON

Ouns, what is the meaning of this?

BEN

Mess, here's the wind changed again. Father, you and I may
make a voyage together now.

ANGELICA

Well, Sir Sampson, since I have played you a trick, I'll   510
advise you how you may avoid such another. Learn to be a
good father, or you'll never get a second wife. I always
loved your son, and hated your unforgiving nature. I was
resolved to try him to the utmost; I have tried you too, and
know you both. You have not more faults than he has   515
virtues; and 'tis hardly more pleasure to me that I can make
him and myself happy, than that I can punish you.

VALENTINE

If my happiness could receive addition, this kind surprise
would make it double.

SIR SAMPSON

Ouns, you're a crocodile.   520

FORESIGHT

Really, Sir Sampson, this is a sudden eclipse –

SIR SAMPSON

You're an illiterate fool, and I'm another, and the stars are
liars; and if I had breath enough, I'd curse them and you,
myself, and everybody. Ouns, cullied, bubbled, jilted,
woman-bobbed at last. – I have not patience.   *Exit*   525

TATTLE

If the gentleman is in this disorder for want of a wife, I can
spare him mine. (*To* JEREMY) O, are you there, sir? I'm
indebted to you for my happiness.

---

522 *illiterate fool* (illiterate old fool Ww)
522–5 *and the stars ... patience* (om. Ww)
524 *cullied ... jilted* deceived
525 s.d. *Exit* (om. Ww)
526 *this disorder* (disorder Ww)

JEREMY

Sir, I ask you ten thousand pardons, 'twas an arrant mistake. You see, sir, my master was never mad, nor anything   530
like it. Then how could it be otherwise?

VALENTINE

Tattle, I thank you, you would have interposed between me
and heaven; but Providence laid purgatory in your way.
You have but justice.

SCANDAL

I hear the fiddles that Sir Sampson provided for his own   535
wedding; methinks 'tis pity they should not be employed
when the match is so much mended. Valentine, though it be
morning, we may have a dance.

VALENTINE

Anything, my friend, everything that looks like joy and
transport.   540

SCANDAL

Call 'em, Jeremy.

ANGELICA

I have done dissembling now, Valentine; and if that cold-
ness which I have always worn before you should turn to
an extreme fondness, you must not suspect it.

VALENTINE

I'll prevent that suspicion, for I intend to dote on at that   545
immoderate rate that your fondness shall never distinguish
itself enough to be taken notice of. If ever you seem to love
too much, it must be only when I can't love enough.

ANGELICA

Have a care of large promises; you know you are apt to run
more in debt than you are able to pay.   550

VALENTINE

Therefore I yield my body as your prisoner, and make your
best on't.

SCANDAL

The music stays for you.

Dance

Well madam, you have done exemplary justice in punishing
an inhuman father, and rewarding a faithful lover; but   555
there is a third good work which I, in particular, must
thank you for: I was an infidel to your sex, and you have
converted me. For now I am convinced that all women are

545–6 *on ... rate* (to that immoderate degree Ww)
549 *large promises* (promises Q3, 4, Ww)
550 *able to pay* (able pay Q1)

not like fortune, blind in bestowing favours, either on those
who do not merit, or who do not want 'em.   560

ANGELICA

'Tis an unreasonable accusation that you lay upon our sex:
you tax us with injustice, only to cover your own want of
merit. You would all have the reward of love, but few have
the constancy to stay till it becomes your due. Men are generally hypocrites and infidels; they pretend to worship, but 565
have neither zeal nor faith. How few, like Valentine, would
persevere even unto martyrdom, and sacrifice their interest
to their constancy! In admiring me, you misplace the
novelty.

    The miracle today is that we find   570
    A lover true: not that a woman's kind.

Exeunt Omnes

567 *unto* (to Ww)

EPILOGUE

Spoken at the opening of the New House,
by Mrs. Bracegirdle

Sure Providence at first designed this place
To be the player's refuge in distress;
For still in every storm they all run hither,
As to a shed that shields 'em from the weather.
But thinking of this change which last befell us,   5
It's like what I have heard our poets tell us:
For when behind our scenes their suits are pleading,
To help their love, sometimes they show their reading;
And wanting ready cash to pay for hearts,
They top their learning on us, and their parts.   10
Once of philosophers they told us stories,
Whom, as I think they called – Py – Pythagories,
I'm sure 'tis some such Latin name they give 'em,
And we, who know no better, must believe 'em.
Now to these men (say they) such souls were given,   15
That after death ne'er went to hell, nor heaven,
But lived, I know not how, in beasts; and then,
When many years were past, in men again.
Methinks we players resemble such a soul,
That does from bodies, we from houses stroll.   20
Thus Aristotle's soul, of old that was,
May now be damned to animate an ass;
Or in this very house, for aught we know,
Is doing painful penance in some beau;
And this our audience, which did once resort   25
To shining theatres to see our sport,
Now find us tossed into a tennis court.
These walls but t'other day were filled with noise
Of roaring gamesters, and your Damme Boys.
Then bounding balls and racquets they encompassed,   30
And now they're filled with jests, and flights, and bombast!
I vow I don't much like this transmigration,
Strolling from place to place, by circulation.

12 *Pythagories* Pythagoras, the *Greek* philosopher who held the doctrine of the
transmigration of souls to which the Epilogue refers
25 *this* (thus Ww)
27 *tennis court* Lisle's tennis court to which the company had removed

Grant heaven, we don't return to our first station.
I know not what these think, but for my part,　　　　35
I can't reflect without an aching heart,
How we should end in our original, a cart.
But we can't fear, since you're so good to save us,
That you have only set us up, to leave us.
Thus from the past, we hope for future grace;　　　　40
I beg it –
And some here know I have a begging face.
Then pray continue this your kind behaviour,
For a clear stage won't do, without your favour.

37　*cart.* i) the cart on which plays were first performed, ii) the cart which conveyed
　　criminals to be hanged
44　*clear stage* a technical term for the stage empty of actors, but implying here free
　　from debt and control